Contents

Low-fat roasties

Prep:10 mins **Cook:**1 hr

Serves 2

Ingredients

- 800g roasting potatoes , quartered
- 1 garlic clove , sliced
- 200ml vegetable stock (from a cube is fine)
- 2 tbsp olive oil

Method

STEP 1

Heat oven to 200C/fan 180C/gas 6. Put the potatoes and garlic in a roasting tin. Pour over the stock, then brush the tops of the potatoes with half the olive oil. Season, then cook for 50 mins. Brush with the remaining oil and cook 10-15 mins more until the stock is absorbed and the potatoes have browned and cooked through.

Smoky spiced veggie rice

Prep:15 mins **Cook:**1 hr

Serves 6

Ingredients

- 25g cashews
- 4 tbsp olive oil
- 1 corn cob
- 250g rainbow baby carrots , halved lengthways
- 2 red onions , finely chopped
- 2 celery sticks , finely chopped
- 2 large red peppers , finely sliced
- 3 garlic cloves , crushed
- 2 tbsp Cajun seasoning
- 1½ tbsp smoked paprika
- 1 tsp chipotle paste
- 2 tbsp tomato purée
- 200g heirloom cherry tomatoes , halved

- 400g can kidney beans , drained and rinsed
- 400g can cherry tomatoes
- 300g long-grain rice , washed
- 400ml vegetable or vegan stock
- 1 tbsp red wine vinegar (vegan varieties are readily available)
- 2 tbsp caster sugar
- 2 spring onions , finely sliced

Method

STEP 1

Dry-fry the cashews in a large saucepan or casserole dish over a medium heat until golden brown. Remove from the heat, leave to cool, then roughly chop. Heat 1 tbsp oil in the same pan over a high heat, then fry the corn on each side for 20 seconds to char. Remove from the pan, set aside, then tip in the carrots and fry for 5 mins. Remove from the pan and set aside.

STEP 2

Heat the rest of the oil in the same pan over a medium heat and fry the onions and celery for 10 mins until soft and slightly coloured. Tip in the peppers and garlic, then fry for another 5 mins before adding the Cajun seasoning, smoked paprika, chipotle paste and tomato purée. Fry for 1 min until the spices are fragrant, then add the cherry tomatoes and fry for another 2 mins.

STEP 3

Stir in the kidney beans, canned tomatoes, rice, stock, vinegar and sugar, then stir until everything is combined. Bring to the boil, then cover with a lid and simmer with a lid on for 35-40 mins on a medium-low heat, stirring halfway through, until the rice is cooked and liquid absorbed.

STEP 4

Slice the corn off the cob and mix it through the rice along with the carrots. Season and garnish with the spring onions and cashews.

Cod puttanesca with spinach & spaghetti

Prep:10 mins **Cook:**17 mins

Serves 2

Ingredients

- 100g wholemeal spaghetti
- 1 large onion , sliced
- 1 tbsp rapeseed oil

- 1 red chilli , deseeded and sliced
- 2 garlic cloves , chopped
- 200g cherry tomatoes , halved
- 1 tsp cider vinegar
- 2 tsp capers
- 5 Kalamata olives , halved
- ½ tsp smoked paprika
- 2 skinless cod fillet or loins
- 160g spinach leaves
- small handful chopped parsley , to serve

Method

STEP 1

Boil the spaghetti for 10 mins until al dente, adding the spinach for the last 2 mins. Meanwhile, fry the onion in the oil in a large non-stick frying pan with a lid until tender and turning golden. Stir in the chilli and garlic, then add the tomatoes.

STEP 2

Add the vinegar, capers, olives and paprika with a ladleful of the pasta water. Put the cod fillets on top, then cover the pan and cook for 5-7 mins until the fish just flakes. Drain the pasta and wilted spinach and pile on to plates, then top with the fish and sauce. Sprinkle over some parsley to serve.

Sesame chicken & prawn skewers

Prep:15 mins **Cook:**5 mins Plus marinating

Makes 20

Ingredients

- thumb-sized piece ginger , grated
- 1 large garlic clove , grated
- 1 tsp honey
- 1½ tsp soy sauce
- 1 tsp sesame oil
- ½ lime , juiced
- 1 tbsp sesame seeds
- 1 skinless chicken breast , cut into 10 pieces
- 10 raw king prawns
- 1 broccoli head , cut into 20 florets

- 20 cocktail skewers

Method

STEP 1

Combine the ginger, garlic, honey, soy sauce, sesame oil, lime juice and sesame seeds. Divide between two bowls, then add the chicken pieces to one and the prawns to the other. Toss both mixtures well, then leave to marinate in the fridge for 15 mins.

STEP 2

Cook the chicken in a frying pan over a medium-high heat for 3 mins, then push to one side and add the prawns to the other side of the pan. Cook for 2 mins until the prawns are pink and the chicken is cooked through (use two separate pans if anyone you're cooking for has an allergy or is a pescatarian). Put the broccoli in a microwaveable bowl with a splash of water, then cover and cook on high for 5 mins.

STEP 3

Thread half of the skewers with chicken and broccoli and the other half with prawns and broccoli.

Charred spring onions & teriyaki tofu

Prep:5 mins **Cook:**25 mins

Serves 2

Ingredients

- 150g wholegrain rice
- 50ml soy sauce
- 2 tbsp mirin
- ½ tsp grated ginger
- 1 tsp honey
- 350g firm tofu (we used Cauldron)
- 1 bunch spring onions , ends trimmed
- 2 tsp sunflower oil
- ½ tsp sesame seeds
- 1 red chilli , sliced (optional)

Method

STEP 1

Cook the rice according to pack instructions. Pour the soy sauce, mirin, ginger and honey into a small saucepan and add 50ml water. Bring to a simmer and cook for around 5 mins or until slightly thickened. Remove from the heat and set aside until needed.

STEP 2

If your tofu doesn't feel very firm, you'll need to press it. To do this, wrap the block of tofu in a few layers of kitchen paper, then weigh it down with a heavy pan or tray for 10-15 mins – the longer you press it, the firmer it will be. Cut the tofu into thick slices.

STEP 3

Heat a griddle pan over high heat and lightly brush the tofu and spring onions with the oil. Griddle the tofu and spring onion until deep char lines appear on both sides (around 4 mins each side) – you may have to do this in batches depending on the size of your griddle pan.

STEP 4

Divide the cooked rice between two plates, top with the tofu and spring onion, then drizzle with the teriyaki sauce. Garnish with the sesame seeds and sliced red chilli, if using.

Hearty pasta soup

Prep:5 mins **Cook:**25 mins

Serves 4

Ingredients

- 1 tbsp olive oil
- 2 carrots, chopped
- 1 large onion, finely chopped
- 1l vegetable stock
- 400g can chopped tomato
- 200g frozen mixed peas and beans
- 250g pack fresh filled tortellini (we used spinach and ricotta)
- handful of basil leaves (optional)
- grated parmesan (or vegetarian alternative), to serve

Method

STEP 1

Heat oil in a pan. Fry the carrots and onion for 5 mins until starting to soften. Add the stock and tomatoes, then simmer for 10 mins. Add the peas and beans with 5 mins to go.

STEP 2

Once veg is tender, stir in the pasta. Return to the boil and simmer for 2 mins until the pasta is just cooked. Stir in the basil, if using. Season, then serve in bowls topped with a sprinkling of Parmesan and slices of garlic bread.

Slow cooker mushroom risotto

Prep:30 mins **Cook:**1 hr

Serves 4

Ingredients

- 1 onion, finely chopped
- 1 tsp olive oil
- 250g chestnut mushrooms, sliced
- 1l vegetable stock
- 50g porcini
- 300g wholegrain rice
- small bunch parsley, finely chopped
- grated vegetarian parmesan-style cheese to serve

Method

STEP 1

Heat the slow cooker if necessary. Fry the onion in the oil in a frying pan with a splash of water for 10 minutes or until it is soft but not coloured. Add the mushroom slices and stir them around until they start to soften and release their juices.

STEP 2

Meanwhile pour the stock into a saucepan and add the porcini, bring to a simmer and then leave to soak. Tip the onions and mushrooms into the slow cooker and add the rice, stir it in well. Pour over the stock and porcini leaving any bits of sediment in the saucepan (or pour the mixture through a fine sieve).

STEP 3

Cook on High for 3 hours, stirring halfway. and then check the consistency – the rice should be cooked. If it needs a little more liquid stir in a splash of stock. Stir in the parsley and season. Serve with the parmesan.

Spicy meatball tagine with bulgur & chickpeas

Prep:10 mins **Cook:**45 mins plus chilling

Serves 4

Ingredients

- 2 onions , 1 quartered, 1 halved and sliced
- 2 tbsp tomato purée
- 2 garlic cloves
- 1 egg
- 1 tbsp chilli powder
- 500g pack extra-lean beef mince
- 2 tsp rapeseed oil
- 4 large carrots , cut into batons
- 1 tsp ground cumin
- 2 tsp ground coriander
- 400g can chopped tomatoes
- 1 lemon , zest removed with a potato peeler, then chopped
- 12 Kalamata olives , chopped
- 1 tbsp vegetable bouillon powder
- ⅓ pack fresh coriander , chopped

For the bulgur

- 200g bulgur wheat
- 400g can chickpeas
- 2 tsp vegetable bouillon powder
- 2 tsp ground coriander

Method

STEP 1

Put the quartered onion in the food processor and process to finely chop it. Add the minced beef, 1 tbsp tomato purée, the garlic, egg and chilli powder and blitz to make a smoothish paste. Divide the mixture into 26 even-sized pieces and roll into balls.

STEP 2

Heat the oil in a large frying pan and cook the meatballs for about 5-10 mins to lightly brown them. Tip from the pan onto a plate.

STEP 3

Now add the sliced onion and carrots to the pan and stir fry briefly in the pan juices to soften them a little. Add the spices and pour in the tomatoes with 1 ½ cans of water then stir in the chopped lemon zest, remaining tomato purée, olives and bouillon powder. Return the meatballs to the pan then cover and cook for 15 mins until the carrots are just tender. Stir in the coriander.

STEP 4

While the tagine is cooking, tip the bulgur into a pan with the chickpeas and water from the can. Add 2 cans of water, the bouillon and coriander. Cover and cook for 10 mins until the bulgur is tender and the liquid had been absorbed. If you're doing the Healthy Diet Plan (serving two people), serve half with half of the tagine and chill the remainder for another night if you like.

Herb & garlic pork with summer ratatouille

Prep:15 mins **Cook:**25 mins

4 (or 2 with leftovers for other meals)

Ingredients

- 2 tsp rapeseed oil
- 2 red onions , halved and sliced
- 2 peppers (any colour), diced
- 1 large aubergine , diced
- 2 large courgettes , halved and sliced
- 2 garlic cloves , chopped
- 400g can chopped tomatoes
- 2 tsp vegetable bouillon
- 1 thyme spig
- handful basil , stalks chopped, leaves torn and kept separate

For the pork

- 475g pork tenderloin, fat trimmed off, cut into 2 equal pieces
- 2 garlic cloves , crushed
- 1 tbsp thyme leaves , plus a few sprigs to decorate
- 1 tsp rapeseed oil
- brown rice or new potatoes, to serve

Method

STEP 1

Heat the oil in a large non-stick pan and fry the onions for 5 mins or until softened. Stir in the peppers, aubergine, courgettes and garlic, and cook, stirring, for a few mins. Tip in the tomatoes and 1 can of water, then stir in the bouillon, thyme and basil stalks. Cover and simmer for 20 mins or until tender. Stir through the basil leaves.

STEP 2

Meanwhile, rub the pork with the garlic, then scatter with the thyme and some black pepper, patting it so it sticks all over. Heat the oil in a non-stick frying pan and cook the pork for about 12 mins, turning frequently so it browns on all sides, until tender but still moist. Cover and rest for 5 mins.

STEP 3

If you're making this as part of the Healthy Diet Plan, set aside half of the pork to use in the curried pork bulghar salad later in the week and store in the fridge once cooled. Chill the half of the ratatouille and use it to make the ratatouille pasta salad with rocket for another day. If you are serving four you can skip this step.

STEP 4

To serve, slice the pork and serve with the ratatouille, some brown rice or new potatoes and some extra thyme.

Summer carrot, tarragon & white bean soup

Prep:10 mins **Cook:**20 mins

Serves 4

Ingredients

- 1 tbsp rapeseed oil
- 2 large leeks , well washed, halved lengthways and finely sliced
- 700g carrots , chopped
- 1.4l hot reduced-salt vegetable bouillon (we used Marigold)
- 4 garlic cloves , finely grated
- 2 x 400g cans cannellini beans in water
- ⅔ small pack tarragon , leaves roughly chopped

Method

STEP 1

Heat the oil over a medium heat in a large pan and fry the leeks and carrots for 5 mins to soften.

STEP 2

Pour over the stock, stir in the garlic, the beans with their liquid, and three-quarters of the tarragon, then cover and simmer for 15 mins or until the veg is just tender. Stir in the remaining tarragon before serving.

Curried fishcake bites

Prep:20 mins **Cook:**15 mins

Makes 24 (12 of each flavour)

Ingredients

- 2 spring onions , trimmed
- 400g skinless cod loin , cubed
- ¼ pack fresh coriander
- 1 large egg
- 2 tsp Madras curry powder
- 1 tsp lemon juice
- 1 tbsp cornflour
- 1 tbsp ground almonds
- rapeseed oil , for frying

For the mango bites

- 12 chunks fresh ripe mango
- 3 thick slices of cucumber , quartered
- For the tomato bites
- 6 cherry tomatoes , halved
- 12 fresh coriander leaves

You will need

- 24 cocktail sticks

Method

STEP 1

Tip the spring onions into a food processor and pulse briefly to chop. Add all the remaining fishcake ingredients, except for the oil, and blitz to a paste. Shape into 24 mini cakes.

STEP 2

Heat a drizzle of the oil in a large non-stick frying pan. Fry half the fishcakes for 1-2 mins each side until firm and golden. Remove from the pan and repeat with the other fishcakes. Will keep in the fridge for up to two days.

STEP 3

To serve, thread the mango and cucumber onto 12 cocktail sticks, then the cherry tomato and a coriander leaf on the remaining sticks. Warm the fishcakes, if you like, at 180C/ 160C fan/gas 4 for 10 mins. Spear the mango version into the side of the fishcakes, then spear the cherry tomato version through the top of the remaining fishcakes.

Singapore chilli crab

Prep:25 mins **Cook:**5 mins

Serves 2

Ingredients

- 1 whole cooked crab (about 1kg)
- 2 tbsp flavourless oil
- 3 garlic cloves , very finely chopped
- thumb-sized piece ginger , very finely chopped
- 3 red chillies , 2 very finely chopped, 1 sliced
- 4 tbsp tomato ketchup
- 2 tbsp soy sauce
- handful coriander leaves, roughly chopped
- 2 spring onions , sliced
- rice or steamed bad buns, to serve

Method

STEP 1

The crab must be prepared before stir-frying (you can ask your fishmonger to do this). This involves removing the claws, the main shell, discarding the dead man's fingers, then cutting the body into four pieces, and cracking the claws and the legs so the sauce can get through to the meat.

STEP 2

Heat the oil in a large wok and sizzle the garlic, ginger and chopped chillies for 1 min or until fragrant. Add the ketchup, soy and 100ml water, and stir to combine. Throw in the crab, turn up the heat and stir-fry for 3-5 mins or until the crab is piping hot and coated in the sauce. Stir through most of the coriander, spring onions and sliced chilli.

STEP 3

Use tongs to arrange the crab on a serving dish, pour over the sauce from the pan and scatter over the remaining coriander, spring onions and sliced chilli. Serve with rice or bao buns, and a lot of napkins.

Lentil fritters

Prep:15 mins **Cook:**10 mins

Serves 2

Ingredients

- 300g leftover basic lentils
- handful of chopped coriander
- 1 chopped spring onion
- 50g gram flour
- 2 carrots
- 2 courgettes
- ½ tsp sesame seeds
- handful of coriander
- ½ tsp sesame oil
- juice of 1 lime
- 1 tbsp rapeseed oil

Method

STEP 1

Mix the leftover lentils with the chopped coriander, spring onion and gram flour, then set aside. Use a peeler to cut the carrots and courgettes into long ribbons, then toss the ribbons with the sesame seeds and coriander in sesame oil and the lime juice.

STEP 2

Heat the rapeseed oil in a frying pan. Spoon in four dollops of the lentil mixture and flatten into patties. Fry each side until golden and serve with the ribbon salad.

Stir-fried pork with ginger & honey

Prep:15 mins **Cook:**10 mins

Serves 2

Ingredients

- 2 nests medium egg noodles
- 2 tsp cornflour
- 2 tbsp soy sauce
- 1 tbsp honey
- 1 tbsp sunflower oil
- 250g/9oz pork tenderloin, cut into bite-sized pieces

- thumb-sized piece ginger, finely chopped
- 2 garlic cloves, finely chopped
- 1 green pepper, deseeded and sliced
- 100g mange tout
- 1 tsp sesame seed

Method

STEP 1

Bring a pan of salted water to the boil and cook the noodles following pack instructions. Meanwhile, mix the cornflour with 1 tbsp water, then stir in the soy sauce and honey, and set aside.

STEP 2

Heat the oil in a wok over a high heat. Add the pork and cook for 2 mins until browned all over. Add the ginger, garlic, pepper and mangetout, and cook for a further 2 mins. Reduce the heat, then add the soy and honey mixture, stirring and cooking until the sauce bubbles and thickens. Divide the drained noodles between 2 bowls. Top with the pork and vegetables, and finish with a sprinkling of sesame seeds.

Prawn tikka masala

Prep:10 mins **Cook:**30 mins

Serves 4

Ingredients

- 1 large onion , roughly chopped
- 1 thumb-sized piece ginger , peeled and grated
- 2 large garlic cloves
- 1 tbsp rapeseed oil
- 2-3 tbsp tikka curry paste
- 400g can chopped tomatoes
- 2 tbsp tomato purée
- ½ tbsp light brown soft sugar
- 3 cardamom pods , bashed
- 200g brown basmati rice
- 3 tbsp ground almonds
- 300g raw king prawns
- 1 tbsp double cream
- ½ bunch of coriander , roughly chopped
- naan breads , warmed, to serve (optional)

Method

STEP 1

Put the onion, ginger and garlic in a food processor and blitz to a smooth paste. Heat the oil in a large flameproof casserole dish or pan over a medium heat. Add the onion paste and fry for 8 mins or until lightly golden. Stir in the curry paste and fry for 1 min more. Add the tomatoes, tomato purée, sugar and cardamom pods. Bring to a simmer and cook, covered, for another 10 mins.

STEP 2

Cook the rice following pack instructions.

STEP 3

Scoop the cardamom out of the curry sauce and discard, then blitz with a hand blender, or in a clean food processor. Return to the pan, add the almonds and prawns, and cook for 5 mins. Season to taste and stir through the cream and coriander. Serve with the rice and naan breads, if you like.

Celery soup

Prep:15 mins **Cook:**40 mins

Serves 3 - 4

Ingredients

- 2 tbsp olive oil
- 300g celery, sliced, with tough strings removed
- 1 garlic clove, peeled
- 200g potatoes, peeled and cut into chunks
- 500ml vegetable stock
- 100ml milk
- crusty bread, to serve

Method

STEP 1

Heat the oil in a large saucepan over a medium heat, tip in the celery, garlic and potatoes and coat in the oil. Add a splash of water and a big pinch of salt and cook, stirring regularly for 15 mins, adding a little more water if the veg begins to stick.

STEP 2

Pour in the vegetable stock and bring to the boil, then turn the heat down and simmer for 20 mins further, until the potatoes are falling apart and the celery is soft. Use a stick blender to purée the soup, then pour in the milk and blitz again. Season to taste. Serve with crusty bread.

Low-fat Spanish omelette

Prep:10 mins **Cook:**15 mins

Serves 1

Ingredients

- 180g sweet potato , peeled and cut into 2cm chunks
- 5ml olive oil
- 55g onion , sliced
- 140g red pepper , diced
- 1 garlic clove , grated
- 5 slices turkey bacon , sliced
- 1 rosemary sprig (optional)
- 5 eggs (1 whole egg and 4 egg whites)
- 2 handfuls green salad leaves
- 150g 0% fat Greek yogurt

Method

STEP 1

Heat oven to 180C/160C fan/gas 4. Heat the sweet potato chunks in the microwave for 3 mins, leave to rest for 2 mins, then heat again for a further 2 mins, by which time they should be cooked through and soft.

STEP 2

Meanwhile, heat the oil in a nonstick ovenproof frying pan over a medium-high heat. Add the onion, pepper, turkey, garlic and rosemary (if using), and cook for 2-3 mins. When the potatoes are ready, add them to the pan as well.

STEP 3

Beat the egg and egg whites together, then pour into the frying pan. Use a spatula to move the eggs around, scraping it up from the base, for 1-2 mins or until there is a good proportion of cooked egg in the pan and the ingredients are well mixed. Put the pan in the oven and heat until the egg is cooked through. Slide the omelette from the pan and enjoy with a side salad and a good dollop of yogurt.

Low-fat turkey bolognese

Prep:10 mins **Cook:**45 mins

Serves 4 - 6

Ingredients

* 400g lean turkey mince (choose breast instead of thigh mince if you can, as it has less fat)
* 2 tsp vegetable oil
* 1 large onion, chopped
* 1 large carrot, chopped
* 3 celery sticks, chopped
* 250g pack brown mushroom, finely chopped
* pinch of sugar
* 1 tbsp tomato purée
* 2 x 400g cans chopped tomato with garlic & herbs
* 400ml chicken stock, made from 1 low-sodium stock cube
* cooked wholemeal pasta and fresh basil leaves (optional), to serve

Method

STEP 1

Heat a large non-stick frying pan and dry-fry the turkey mince until browned. Tip onto a plate and set aside.

STEP 2

Add the oil and gently cook the onion, carrot and celery until softened, about 10 mins (add a splash of water if it starts to stick). Add the mushrooms and cook for a few mins, then add the sugar and tomato purée, and cook for 1 min more, stirring to stop it from sticking.

STEP 3

Add the tomatoes, turkey and stock with some seasoning. Simmer for at least 20 mins (or longer) until thickened. Serve with the pasta and fresh basil, if you have it.

Low-fat chicken biryani

Prep:25 mins **Cook:**1 hr and 35 mins Plus marinating

Serves 5

Ingredients

* 3 garlic cloves , finely grated
* 2 tsp finely grated ginger

- ¼ tsp ground cinnamon
- 1 tsp turmeric
- 5 tbsp natural yogurt
- 600g boneless, skinless chicken breast , cut into 4-5cm pieces
- 2 tbsp semi-skimmed milk
- good pinch saffron
- 4 medium onions
- 4 tbsp rapeseed oil
- ½ tsp hot chilli powder
- 1 cinnamon stick , broken in half
- 5 green cardamom pods , lightly bashed to split
- 3 cloves
- 1 tsp cumin seed
- 280g basmati rice
- 700ml chicken stock
- 1 tsp garam masala
- handful chopped coriander leaves

Method

STEP 1

In a mixing bowl, stir together the garlic, ginger, cinnamon, turmeric and yogurt with some pepper and ¼ tsp salt. Tip in the chicken pieces and stir to coat (see **step 1**, above). Cover and marinate in the fridge for about 1 hr or longer if you have time. Warm the milk to tepid, stir in the saffron and set aside.

STEP 2

Heat oven to 200C/180C fan/gas 6. Slice each onion in half lengthways, reserve half and cut the other half into thin slices. Pour 1½ tbsp of the oil onto a baking tray, scatter over the sliced onion, toss to coat, then spread out in a thin, even layer (**step 2**). Roast for 40-45 mins, stirring halfway, until golden.

STEP 3

When the chicken has marinated, thinly slice the reserved onion. Heat 1 tbsp oil in a large sauté or frying pan. Fry the onion for 4-5 mins until golden. Stir in the chicken, a spoonful at a time, frying until it is no longer opaque, before adding the next spoonful (this helps to prevent the yogurt from curdling). Once the last of the chicken has been added, stir-fry for a further 5 mins until everything looks juicy. Scrape any sticky bits off the bottom of the pan, stir in the chilli powder, then pour in 100ml water, cover and simmer on a low heat for 15 mins. Remove and set aside.

STEP 4

Cook the rice while the chicken simmers. Heat another 1 tbsp oil in a large sauté pan, then drop in the cinnamon stick, cardamom, cloves and cumin seeds. Fry briefly until their aroma is released. Tip in the rice (**step 3**) and fry for 1 min, stirring constantly. Stir in the stock and bring to the boil. Lower the heat and simmer, covered, for about 8 mins or until all the stock has been absorbed. Remove from the heat and leave with the lid on for a few mins, so the rice can fluff up. Stir the garam masala into the remaining 1½ tsp oil and set aside. When the onions are roasted, remove and reduce oven to 180C/160C fan/gas 4.

STEP 5

Spoon half the chicken and its juices into an ovenproof dish, about 25 x 18 x 6cm, then scatter over a third of the roasted onions. Remove the whole spices from the rice, then layer half of the rice over the chicken and onions. Drizzle over the spiced oil. Spoon over the rest of the chicken and a third more onions. Top with the remaining rice (**step 4**) and drizzle over the saffron-infused milk. Scatter over the rest of the onions, cover tightly with foil and heat through in the oven for about 25 mins. Serve scattered with the mint and coriander.

Low-fat moussaka

Prep: 15 mins **Cook:** 40 mins

Serves 4

Ingredients

- 200g frozen sliced peppers
- 3 garlic cloves , crushed
- 200g extra-lean minced beef
- 100g red lentils
- 2 tsp dried oregano , plus extra for sprinkling
- 500ml carton passata
- 1 aubergine , sliced into 1.5cm rounds
- 4 tomatoes , sliced into 1cm rounds
- 2 tsp olive oil
- 25g parmesan , finely grated
- 170g pot 0% fat Greek yogurt
- freshly grated nutmeg

Method

STEP 1

Cook the peppers gently in a large non-stick pan for about 5 mins – the water from them should stop them sticking. Add the garlic and cook for 1 min more, then add the beef, breaking up with a fork, and cook until brown. Tip in the lentils, half the oregano, the passata and a splash of water. Simmer for 15-20 mins until the lentils are tender, adding more water if you need to.

STEP 2

Meanwhile, heat the grill to Medium. Arrange the aubergine and tomato slices on a non-stick baking tray and brush with the oil. Sprinkle with the remaining oregano and some seasoning, then grill for 1-2 mins each side until lightly charred – you may need to do this in batches.

STEP 3

Mix half the Parmesan with the yogurt and some seasoning. Divide the beef mixture between 4 small ovenproof dishes and top with the sliced aubergine and tomato. Spoon over the yogurt topping and sprinkle with the extra oregano, Parmesan and nutmeg. Grill for 3-4 mins until bubbling. Serve with a salad, if you like.

Mushroom stroganoff

Prep:10 mins **Cook:**20 mins

Serves 2

Ingredients

- 2 tsp olive oil
- 1 onion, finely chopped
- 1 tbsp paprika
- 2 garlic cloves, crushed
- 300g mixed mushrooms, chopped
- 150ml low-sodium beef or vegetable stock
- 1 tbsp Worcestershire sauce, or vegetarian alternative
- 3 tbsp half-fat soured cream
- small bunch of parsley, roughly chopped
- 250g pouch cooked wild rice

Method

STEP 1

Heat the olive oil in a large non-stick frying pan and soften the onion for about 5 mins.

STEP 2

Add the paprika and garlic, then cook for 1 min more. Add the mushrooms and cook on a high heat, stirring often, for about 5 mins.

STEP 3

Pour in the stock and Worcestershire sauce. Bring to the boil, bubble for 5 mins until the sauce thickens, then turn off the heat and stir through the soured cream and most of the parsley. Make sure the pan is not on the heat or the sauce may split.

STEP 4

Heat the wild rice following pack instructions, then stir through the remaining chopped parsley and serve with the stroganoff.

20-minute seafood pasta

Total time20 mins Ready in 20 mins

Serves 4

Ingredients

- 1 tbsp olive oil
- 1 onion, chopped
- 1 garlic clove, chopped
- 1 tsp paprika
- 400g can chopped tomatoes
- 1l chicken stock (from a cube is fine)
- 300g spaghetti, roughly broken
- 240g frozen seafood mix, defrosted
- handful of parsley leaves, chopped, and lemon wedges, to serve

Method

STEP 1

Heat the oil in a wok or large frying pan, then cook the onion and garlic over a medium heat for 5 mins until soft. Add the paprika, tomatoes and stock, then bring to the boil.

STEP 2

Turn down the heat to a simmer, stir in the pasta and cook for 7 mins, stirring occasionally to stop the pasta from sticking. Stir in the seafood, cook for 3 mins more until it's all heated through and the pasta is cooked, then season to taste. Sprinkle with the parsley and serve with lemon wedges.

Low-fat cherry cheesecake

Prep:1 hr **Cook:**30 mins Plus overnight chilling

Ingredients

- 25g butter , melted
- 140g amaretti biscuit , crushed
- 3 sheets leaf gelatine
- zest and juice 1 orange
- 2 x 250g tubs quark
- 250g tub ricotta
- 2 tsp vanilla extract
- 100g icing sugar

For the topping

- 400g fresh cherry , stoned
- 5 tbsp cherry jam
- 1 tbsp cornflour

Method

STEP 1

Line the sides of a 20cm round loose-bottomed cake tin with baking parchment. Stir the butter into twothirds of the biscuit crumbs, and reserve the rest. Sprinkle the buttery crumbs over the base of the tin and press down. Soak the gelatine in cold water for 5-10 mins until soft.

STEP 2

Warm the orange juice in a small pan or the microwave until almost boiling. Squeeze the gelatine of excess water, then stir into the juice to dissolve.

STEP 3

Beat the quark, ricotta, vanilla and icing sugar together with an electric whisk until really smooth. Then, with the beaters still running, pour in the juice mixture and beat to combine. Pour the cheesecake mixture over the crumbs and smooth the top. Cover with cling film and chill overnight.

STEP 4

To make the topping, put the cherries in a pan with the orange zest and 100ml water. Cook, covered, for 15 mins until the cherries are softened. Put one-third of the cherries in a bowl and mash with a potato masher to give you a chunky compote. Return to the pan, add the jam, cornflour and 2 tbsp water, and mix to combine. Cook until thickened and saucy – if the sauce is too dry, add a splash more water. Cool to room temperature.

STEP 5

Just before serving, carefully remove the cheesecake from the tin and peel off the parchment. Scatter over the remaining biscuit crumbs and some cherry sauce. Serve in slices with the remaining cherry sauce alongside.

Chilli prawn linguine

Prep:5 mins **Cook:**20 mins - 25 mins

Serves 6

Ingredients

- 280g linguine pasta
- 200g sugar snap peas, trimmed
- 2 tbsp olive oil
- 2 large garlic cloves, finely chopped
- 1 large red chilli, deseeded and finely chopped
- 24 raw king prawns, peeled
- 12 cherry tomatoes, halved
- a handful of fresh basil leaves
- mixed salad leaves and crusty white bread, to serve
- For the lime dressing
- 2 tbsp virtually fat-free fromage frais
- grated zest and juice of 2 limes
- 2 tsp golden caster sugar

Method

STEP 1

To make the dressing, mix 2 tbsp virtually fat-free fromage frais, the grated zest and juice of 2 limes and 2 tsp golden caster sugar in a small bowl and season with salt and pepper. Set aside.

STEP 2

Cook 280g linguine pasta according to the packet instructions. Add 200g trimmed sugar snap peas for the last minute or so of cooking time.

STEP 3

Meanwhile, heat 2 tbsp olive oil in a wok or big frying pan, toss in 2 finely chopped large garlic cloves and 1 deseeded and finely chopped large red chilli and cook over a fairly gentle heat for about 30 seconds without letting the garlic brown.

STEP 4

Tip in 24 peeled raw king prawns and cook over a high heat, stirring frequently, for about 3 minutes until they turn pink.

STEP 5

Add 12 halved cherry tomatoes and cook, stirring occasionally, for 3 minutes until they just start to soften.

STEP 6

Drain the linguine pasta and sugar snap peas well, then toss into the prawn mixture.

STEP 7

Tear in a handful of basil leaves, stir, and season with salt and pepper.

STEP 8

Serve with mixed salad leaves drizzled with the lime dressing, and warm crusty white bread.

Spinach, sweet potato & lentil dhal

Prep:10 mins **Cook:**35 mins

Serves 4

Ingredients

- 1 tbsp sesame oil
- 1 red onion, finely chopped
- 1 garlic clove, crushed
- thumb-sized piece ginger, peeled and finely chopped
- 1 red chilli, finely chopped
- 1 ½ tsp ground turmeric
- 1 ½ tsp ground cumin
- 2 sweet potatoes (about 400g/14oz), cut into even chunks
- 250g red split lentils
- 600ml vegetable stock
- 80g bag of spinach
- 4 spring onions, sliced on the diagonal, to serve
- ½ small pack of Thai basil, leaves torn, to serve

Method

STEP 1

Heat 1 tbsp sesame oil in a wide-based pan with a tight-fitting lid.

STEP 2

Add 1 finely chopped red onion and cook over a low heat for 10 mins, stirring occasionally, until softened.

STEP 3

Add 1 crushed garlic clove, a finely chopped thumb-sized piece of ginger and 1 finely chopped red chilli, cook for 1 min, then add 1 ½ tsp ground turmeric and 1 ½ tsp ground cumin and cook for 1 min more.

STEP 4

Turn up the heat to medium, add 2 sweet potatoes, cut into even chunks, and stir everything together so the potato is coated in the spice mixture.

STEP 5

Tip in 250g red split lentils, 600ml vegetable stock and some seasoning.

STEP 6

Bring the liquid to the boil, then reduce the heat, cover and cook for 20 mins until the lentils are tender and the potato is just holding its shape.

STEP 7

Taste and adjust the seasoning, then gently stir in the 80g spinach. Once wilted, top with the 4 diagonally sliced spring onions and ½ small pack torn basil leaves to serve.

STEP 8

Alternatively, allow to cool completely, then divide between airtight containers and store in the fridge for a healthy lunchbox.

West Indian spiced aubergine curry

Prep:30 mins **Cook:**15 mins

Serves 2

Ingredients

- 1 tsp ground cumin
- 1 tsp ground coriander
- ½ tsp ground turmeric
- 1 large aubergine
- 2 tbsp tomato purée
- ½ green chilli , finely chopped

- 1cm piece ginger , peeled and finely chopped
- 2 tsp caster sugar
- ½-1 tbsp rapeseed oil
- 3 spring onions , chopped
- ½ bunch of coriander , shredded
- cooked rice , natural yogurt, roti and lime wedges, to serve

Method

STEP 1

Mix the dry spices and 1 tsp salt together in a bowl and set aside.

STEP 2

Slice the aubergine into 1cm rounds, then score both sides of each round with the tip of a sharp knife. Rub with the spice mix until well coated (you should use all of the mix), then transfer to a board. Put 150ml water in the empty spice bowl with the tomato purée, chilli, ginger and sugar. Set aside.

STEP 3

Heat the oil in a large non-stick frying pan over a medium heat and arrange the aubergine in the pan, overlapping the rounds if needed. Fry for 5 mins on each side, or until golden. Add the liquid mix from the bowl, bring to a simmer, cover and cook for 15-20 mins, turning the aubergine occasionally until it's cooked through. If it seems dry, you may need to add up to 100ml more water to make it saucier. Season.

STEP 4

Scatter over the spring onions and coriander, and serve with rice, yogurt, roti and lime wedges for squeezing over.

Golden goose fat potatoes & parsnips

Prep:15 mins **Cook:**2 hrs and 10 mins

Serves 6

Ingredients

- 1 ½kg Maris Piper potatoes , cut into large chunks
- 600g parsnips , peeled and cut into large chunks
- 100g goose fat
- handful rosemary sprigs (optional)

Method

STEP 1

Tip the potatoes into a large pan of cold salted water and bring to the boil. Turn the heat down slightly and keep the water bubbling gently for 3 mins, then add the parsnips and continue to simmer for 3 mins more. Drain everything and leave until cool enough to handle, then separate the parsnips and the potatoes.

STEP 2

Heat oven to 200C/180C fan/gas 6 with a large roasting tin containing the goose fat inside. When the goose fat is hot, remove the tin from the oven. Carefully tip in the potatoes and turn them so they're completely coated in fat. Place the tin back in the oven and leave undisturbed for 1 hr. Remove the tin from the oven, add the parsnips and gently turn everything together.

STEP 3

Increase oven temperature to 220C/200C fan/gas 8. Roast everything for 20 mins, then turn the parsnips and potatoes again with the rosemary, if using, and roast for about another 15 mins until everything is golden and crisp. Sprinkle with sea salt and scoop into a warm serving dish.

Soup maker tomato soup

Prep:5 mins **Cook:**30 mins

Serves 2

Ingredients

- 500g ripe tomatoes , off the vine and quartered or halved
- 1 small onion , chopped
- ½ small carrot , chopped
- ½ celery stick, chopped
- 1 tsp tomato purée
- pinch of sugar
- 450ml vegetable stock

Method

STEP 1

Put all the ingredients into the soup maker and press the 'smooth soup' function. Make sure you don't fill the soup maker above the max fill line.

STEP 2

Once the cycle is complete, season well, and check the soup for sweetness. Add a little more sugar, salt or tomato puree for depth of colour, if you like.

Slow cooker lasagne

Prep:1 hr and 15 mins **Cook:**3 hrs

Serves 4

Ingredients

- 2 tsp rapeseed oil
- 2 onions, finely chopped
- 4 celery sticks (about 175g), finely diced
- 4 carrots (320g), finely diced
- 2 garlic cloves, chopped
- 400g lean (5% fat) mince beef
- 400g can chopped tomatoes
- 2 tbsp tomato purée
- 2 tsp vegetable bouillon
- 1 tbsp balsamic vinegar
- 1 tbsp fresh thyme leaves
- 6 wholewheat lasagne sheets (105g)

For the sauce

- 400ml whole milk
- 50g wholemeal flour
- 1 bay leaf
- generous grating of nutmeg
- 15g finely grated parmesan

Method

STEP 1

Heat the slow cooker if necessary. Heat the oil in a large non-stick pan and fry the onions, celery, carrots and garlic for 5-10 mins, stirring frequently until softened and starting to colour. Tip in the meat and break it down with a wooden spoon, stirring until it browns. Pour in the tomatoes with a quarter of a can of water, the tomato purée, bouillon, balsamic vinegar, thyme and plenty of black pepper, return to the boil and cook for 5 mins more.

STEP 2

Spoon half the mince in the slow cooker and top with half the lasagne, breaking it where necessary so it covers as much of the meat layer as possible. Top with the rest of the meat, and then another layer of the lasagne. Cover and cook on Low while you make the sauce.

STEP 3

Tip the milk and flour into a pan with the bay leaf and nutmeg and cook on the hob, whisking continuously until thickened. Carry on cooking for a few mins to cook the flour. Remove the bay leaf and stir in the cheese. Pour onto the pasta and spread out with a spatula, then cover and cook for 3 hours until the meat is cooked and the pasta is tender. Allow to settle for 10 mins before serving with salad.

Turkey meatloaf

Prep:15 mins **Cook:**55 mins

Serves 4

Ingredients

- 1 tbsp olive oil
- 1 large onion , finely chopped
- 1 garlic clove , crushed
- 2 tbsp Worcestershire sauce
- 2 tsp tomato purée , plus 1 tbsp for the beans
- 500g turkey mince (thigh is best)
- 1 large egg , beaten
- 85g fresh white breadcrumbs
- 2 tbsp barbecue sauce , plus 4 tbsp for the beans
- 2 x 400g cans cannellini beans
- 1-2 tbsp roughly chopped parsley

Method

STEP 1

Heat oven to 180C/160C fan/gas 4. Heat the oil in a large frying pan and cook the onion for 8-10 mins until softened. Add the garlic, Worcestershire sauce and 2 tsp tomato purée, and stir until combined. Set aside to cool.

STEP 2

Put the turkey mince, egg, breadcrumbs and cooled onion mix in a large bowl and season well. Mix everything to combine, then shape into a rectangular loaf and place in a large roasting tin. Spread 2 tbsp barbecue sauce over the meatloaf and bake for 30 mins.

STEP 3

Meanwhile, drain 1 can of beans only, then pour both cans into a large bowl. Add the remaining barbecue sauce and tomato purée. Season and set aside.

STEP 4

When the meatloaf has had its initial cooking time, scatter the beans around the outside and bake for 15 mins more until the meatloaf is cooked through and the beans are piping hot. Scatter over the parsley and serve the meatloaf in slices.

All-in–one chicken with wilted spinach

Prep:20 mins **Cook:**1 hr

Serves 2

Ingredients

- 2 beetroot , peeled and cut into small chunks
- 300g celeriac , cut into small chunks
- 2 red onions , quartered
- 8 garlic cloves , 4 crushed, the rest left whole, but peeled
- 1 tbsp rapeseed oil
- 1½ tbsp fresh thyme leaves , plus extra to serve
- 1 lemon , zested and juiced
- 1 tsp fennel seeds
- 1 tsp English mustard powder
- 1 tsp smoked paprika
- 4 tbsp bio yogurt
- 4 bone-in chicken thighs , skin removed
- 260g bag spinach

Method

STEP 1

Heat oven to 200C/180C fan/gas 6. Tip the beetroot, celeriac, onions and whole garlic cloves into a shallow roasting tin. Add the oil, 1 tbsp thyme, half the lemon zest, fennel seeds and a squeeze of lemon juice, then toss together. Roast for 20 mins while you prepare the chicken.

STEP 2

Stir the mustard powder and paprika into 2 tbsp yogurt in a bowl. Add half the crushed garlic, the remaining lemon zest and thyme, and juice from half the lemon. Add the chicken and toss well until it's coated all over. Put the chicken in the tin with the veg and roast for 40 mins until the chicken is cooked through and the vegetables are tender.

STEP 3

About 5 mins before the chicken is ready, wash and drain the spinach and put it in a pan with the remaining crushed garlic. Cook until wilted, then turn off the heat and stir in the remaining yogurt. Scatter some extra thyme over the chicken and vegetables, then serve.

Green chowder with prawns

Prep:10 mins **Cook:**20 mins - 30 mins

Serves 4

Ingredients

- 1 tbsp olive oil
- 1 onion , finely chopped
- 1 celery stick , finely chopped
- 1 garlic clove
- 300g petit pois
- 200g pack sliced kale
- 2 potatoes , finely chopped
- 1 low-salt chicken stock cube (we used Kallo)
- 100g cooked North Atlantic prawns

Method

STEP 1

Heat the oil in a saucepan over a medium heat. Add the onion and celery and cook for 5-6 mins until softened but not coloured. Add the garlic and cook for a further min. Stir in the petit pois, kale and potatoes, then add the stock cube and 750ml water. Bring to the boil and simmer for 10-12 mins until the potatoes are soft.

STEP 2

Tip ¾ of the mixture into a food processor and whizz until smooth. Add a little more water or stock if it's too thick. Pour the mixture back into the pan and add half the prawns.

STEP 3

Divide between four bowls and spoon the remaining prawns on top. *Can be frozen for up to a month. Add the prawns once defrosted.*

Easy chicken stew

Prep:10 mins **Cook:**50 mins

Serves 4

Ingredients

- 1 tbsp olive oil
- 1 bunch spring onions , sliced, white and green parts separated
- 1 small swede (350g), peeled and chopped into small pieces
- 400g potatoes , peeled and chopped into small pieces
- 8 skinless boneless chicken thighs
- 1 tbsp Dijon mustard
- 500ml chicken stock
- 200g Savoy cabbage or spring cabbage, sliced
- 2 tsp cornflour (optional)
- crusty bread or cheese scones, to serve (optional)

Method

STEP 1

Heat the oil in a large saucepan. Add the white spring onion slices and fry for 1 min to soften. Tip in the swede and potatoes and cook for 2-3 mins more, then add the chicken, mustard and stock. Cover and cook for 35 mins, or until the vegetables are tender and the chicken cooked through.

STEP 2

Add the cabbage and simmer for another 5 mins. If the stew looks too thin, mix the cornflour with 1 tbsp cold water and pour a couple of teaspoonfuls into the pan; let the stew bubble and thicken, then check again. If it's still too thin, add a little more of the cornflour mix and let the stew bubble and thicken some more.

STEP 3

Season to taste, then spoon the stew into deep bowls. Scatter over the green spring onion slices and serve with crusty bread or warm cheese scones, if you like.

Healthy bolognese

Prep:5 mins **Cook:**20 mins

2 generously, 4 as a snack

Ingredients

- 100g wholewheat linguine
- 2 tsp rapeseed oil
- 1 fennel bulb , finely chopped

- 2 garlic cloves , sliced
- 200g pork mince with less than 5% fat
- 200g whole cherry tomatoes
- 1 tbsp balsamic vinegar
- 1 tsp vegetable bouillon powder
- generous handful chopped basil

Method

STEP 1

Bring a large pan of water to the boil, then cook the linguine following pack instructions, about 10 mins.

STEP 2

Meanwhile, heat the oil in a non-stick wok or wide pan. Add the fennel and garlic and cook, stirring every now and then, until tender, about 10 mins.

STEP 3

Tip in the pork and stir-fry until it changes colour, breaking it up as you go so there are no large clumps. Add the tomatoes, vinegar and bouillon, then cover the pan and cook for 10 mins over a low heat until the tomatoes burst and the pork is cooked and tender. Add the linguine and basil and plenty of pepper, and toss well before serving.

Fennel spaghetti

Prep:15 mins **Cook:**30 mins

Serves 2

Ingredients

- 1 tbsp olive oil , plus extra for serving
- 1 tsp fennel seeds
- 2 small garlic cloves , 1 crushed, 1 thinly sliced
- 1 lemon , zested and juiced
- 1 fennel bulb , finely sliced, fronds reserved
- 150g spaghetti
- ½ pack flat-leaf parsley , chopped
- shaved parmesan (or vegetarian alternative), to serve (optional)

Method

STEP 1

Heat the oil in a frying pan over a medium heat and cook the fennel seeds until they pop. Sizzle the garlic for 1 min, then add the lemon zest and half the fennel slices. Cook for 10-12 mins or until the fennel has softened.

STEP 2

Meanwhile, bring a pan of salted water to the boil and cook the pasta for 1 min less than pack instructions. Use tongs to transfer the pasta to the frying pan along with a good splash of pasta water. Increase the heat to high and toss well. Stir through the remaining fennel slices, the parsley and lemon juice, season generously, then tip straight into two bowls to serve. Top with the fennel fronds, extra olive oil and parmesan shavings, if you like.

Carrot & ginger soup

Prep:15 mins **Cook:**25 mins - 30 mins

Serves 4

Ingredients

- 1 tbsp rapeseed oil
- 1 large onion, chopped
- 2 tbsp coarsely grated ginger
- 2 garlic cloves, sliced
- ½ tsp ground nutmeg
- 850ml vegetable stock
- 500g carrot (preferably organic), sliced
- 400g can cannellini beans (no need to drain)

Supercharged topping

- 4 tbsp almonds in their skins, cut into slivers
- sprinkle of nutmeg

Method

STEP 1

Heat the oil in a large pan, add the onion, ginger and garlic, and fry for 5 mins until starting to soften. Stir in the nutmeg and cook for 1 min more.

STEP 2

Pour in the stock, add the carrots, beans and their liquid, then cover and simmer for 20-25 mins until the carrots are tender.

STEP 3

Scoop a third of the mixture into a bowl and blitz the remainder with a hand blender or in a food processor until smooth. Return everything to the pan and heat until bubbling. Serve topped with the almonds and nutmeg.

Thai prawn & ginger noodles

Prep: 15 mins **Cook:** 15 mins plus soaking

Serves 2

Ingredients

- 100g folded rice noodles (sen lek)
- zest and juice 1 small orange
- 1½-2 tbsp red curry paste
- 1-2 tsp fish sauce
- 2 tsp light brown soft sugar
- 1 tbsp sunflower oil
- 25g ginger, scraped and shredded
- 2 large garlic cloves, sliced
- 1 red pepper, deseeded and sliced
- 85g sugar snap peas, halved lengthways
- 140g beansprouts
- 175g pack raw king prawns
- handful chopped basil
- handful chopped coriander

Method

STEP 1

Put the noodles in a bowl and pour over boiling water to cover them. Set aside to soak for 10 mins. Stir together the orange juice and zest, curry paste, fish sauce, sugar and 3 tbsp water to make a sauce.

STEP 2

Heat the oil in a large wok and add half the ginger and the garlic. Cook, stirring, for 1 min. Add the pepper and stir-fry for 3 mins more. Toss in the sugar snaps, cook briefly, then pour in the curry sauce. Add the beansprouts and prawns, and continue cooking until the prawns just turn pink. Drain the noodles, then toss these into the pan with the herbs and remaining ginger. Mix until the noodles are well coated in the sauce, then serve.

Squash & spinach fusilli with pecans

Prep:10 mins **Cook:**40 mins

Serves 2

Ingredients

- 160g butternut squash , diced
- 3 garlic cloves , sliced
- 1 tbsp chopped sage leaves
- 2 tsp rapeseed oil
- 1 large courgette , halved and sliced
- 6 pecan halves
- 115g wholemeal fusilli
- 125g bag baby spinach

Method

STEP 1

Heat oven to 200C/180C fan/gas 6. Toss the butternut squash, garlic and sage in the oil, then spread out in a roasting tin and cook in the oven for 20 mins, add the courgettes and cook for a further 15 mins. Give everything a stir, then add the pecans and cook for 5 mins more until the nuts are toasted and the vegetables are tender and starting to caramelise.

STEP 2

Meanwhile, boil the pasta according to pack instructions – about 12 mins. Drain, then tip into a serving bowl and toss with the spinach so that it wilts in the heat from the pasta. Add the roasted veg and pecans, breaking up the nuts a little, and toss again really well before serving.

Lighter chicken cacciatore

Prep:15 mins **Cook:**50 mins

Serves 4

Ingredients

- 1 tbsp olive oil
- 3 slices prosciutto, fat removed, chopped
- 1 medium onion, chopped
- 2 garlic cloves, finely chopped

- 2 sage sprigs
- 2 rosemary sprigs
- 4 skinless chicken breasts (550g total weight), preferably organic
- 150ml dry white wine
- 400g can plum tomatoes in natural juice
- 1 tbsp tomato purée
- 225g chestnut mushrooms, quartered or halved if large
- small handful chopped flat-leaf parsley, to serve

Method

STEP 1

Heat the oil in a large non-stick frying pan. Tip in the prosciutto and fry for about 2 mins until crisp. Remove with a slotted spoon, letting any fat drain back into the pan, and set aside. Put the onion, garlic and herbs in the pan and fry for 3-4 mins.

STEP 2

Spread the onion out in the pan, then lay the chicken breasts on top. Season with pepper and fry for 5 mins over a medium heat, turning the chicken once, until starting to brown on both sides and the onion is caramelising on the bottom of the pan. Remove the chicken and set aside on a plate. Raise the heat, give it a quick stir and, when sizzling, pour in the wine and let it bubble for 2 mins to reduce slightly.

STEP 3

Lower the heat to medium, return the prosciutto to the pan, then stir in the tomatoes (breaking them up with your spoon), tomato purée and mushrooms. Spoon 4 tbsp of water into the empty tomato can, swirl it around, then pour it into the pan. Cover and simmer for 15-20 mins or until the sauce has thickened and reduced slightly, then return the chicken to the pan and cook, uncovered, for about 15 mins or until the chicken is cooked through. Season and scatter over the parsley to serve.

Peri-peri chicken pilaf

Prep:20 mins **Cook:**40 mins

Serves 4

Ingredients

- 1 tbsp olive oil
- pack of 6 skinless boneless chicken thighs , cut into large chunks
- 2 tbsp peri-peri seasoning
- 1 onion , finely chopped
- 2 garlic cloves , crushed

- 350g basmati rice
- 500ml hot chicken stock
- 3 peppers (any colour you like), sliced into strips
- 3 large tomatoes , deseeded and roughly chopped
- small pack parsley , roughly chopped
- 2 red chillies , sliced (optional)
- ½ lemon , cut into wedges, to serve

Method

STEP 1

Heat the oil in a large pan over a medium heat. Rub the chicken with 1 tbsp of the peri-peri and brown in the pan for 1 min each side until golden. Transfer to a plate and set aside.

STEP 2

Add the onion to the pan and cook on a gentle heat for 8-10 mins until soft. Add the garlic and remaining peri-peri, and give everything a stir. Tip in the rice and stir to coat.

STEP 3

Add the stock and return the chicken to the pan. Add the peppers and cover with a lid, then simmer gently for 25 mins until cooked. About 5 mins before the end of cooking, add the tomatoes.

STEP 4

Stir through the parsley, scatter over the chillies (if you like it spicy) and serve with lemon wedges.

Chicken & sweetcorn soup

Prep:10 mins **Cook:**2 hrs and 15 mins

Serves 2

Ingredients

- 1 chicken carcass
- 4 thin slices fresh ginger, plus 1 tbsp finely grated
- 2 onions, quartered
- 3 garlic cloves, finely grated
- 2 tsp apple cider vinegar
- 325g can sweetcorn
- 3 spring onions, whites thinly sliced, greens sliced at an angle
- 100g cooked chicken, shredded

- 2 tsp tamari
- 2 eggs, beaten
- few drops sesame oil, to serve (optional)

Method

STEP 1

Boil a large kettle of water. Break the carcass into a big non-stick pan and add the ginger slices, onion and two-thirds of the garlic. Cook, stirring, for about 2 mins – the meat will stick to the base of the pan, but this will add to the flavour. Pour in 1.5 litres of boiling water, stir in the vinegar, then cover and simmer for 2 hrs.

STEP 2

Put a large sieve over a bowl and pour through the contents of the pan. Measure the liquid in the bowl – you want around 450ml. If you have too much, return to the pan and boil with the lid off to reduce it. Transfer the onion from the sieve to a bowl with three-quarters of the sweetcorn. Blitz until smooth with a hand blender.

STEP 3

Return the broth to the pan, and tip in the puréed corn, remaining sweetcorn and garlic, the grated ginger, the whites of the spring onions and the chicken. Simmer for 5 mins, then stir in the tamari. Turn off the heat, and quickly drizzle in the egg, stirring a little to create egg threads. Season with pepper, then ladle into the bowls. Top with the spring onion greens and a few drops of sesame oil, if using.

Vegan bolognese

Prep:20 mins **Cook:**1 hr

Serves 3

Ingredients

- 15g dried porcini mushrooms
- 1 ½ tbsp olive oil
- ½ onion, finely chopped
- 1 carrot, finely chopped
- 1 celery stick, finely chopped
- 2 garlic cloves, sliced
- 2 thyme sprigs
- ½ tsp tomato purée
- 50ml vegan red wine (optional)
- 125g dried green lentils

- 400g can whole plum tomatoes
- 125g chestnut mushrooms, chopped
- 125g portobello mushrooms, sliced
- ½ tsp soy sauce
- ½ tsp Marmite
- 270g spaghetti
- handful fresh basil leaves

Method

STEP 1

Pour 400ml boiling water over the dried porcini and leave for 10 mins until hydrated. Meanwhile pour 1 tbsp oil into a large saucepan. Add the onion, carrot, celery and a pinch of salt. Cook gently, stirring for 10 mins until soft. Remove the porcini from the liquid, keeping the mushroomy stock and roughly chop. Set both aside.

STEP 2

Add the garlic and thyme to the pan. Cook for 1 min then stir in the tomato purée and cook for a min more. Pour in the red wine, if using, cook until nearly reduced, then add the lentils, reserved mushroom stock and tomatoes. Bring to the boil, then reduce the heat and leave to simmer with a lid on.

STEP 3

Meanwhile, heat a large frying pan. Add the remaining oil, then tip in the chestnut, portobello and rehydrated mushrooms. Fry until all the water has evaporated and the mushrooms are deep golden brown. Pour in the soy sauce. Give everything a good mix, then scrape the mushrooms into the lentil mixture.

STEP 4

Stir in the Marmite and continue to cook the ragu, stirring occasionally, over a low-medium heat for 30-45 mins until the lentils are cooked and the sauce is thick and reduced, adding extra water if necessary. Remove the thyme sprigs and season to taste.

STEP 5

Cook the spaghetti in a large pan of salted water for 1 min less than packet instructions. Drain the pasta, reserving a ladleful of pasta water, then toss the spaghetti in the sauce, using a little of the starchy liquid to loosen up the ragu slightly so that the pasta clings to the sauce. Serve topped with fresh basil and some black pepper.

Samosa pie

Prep:5 mins **Cook:**30 mins

Serves 4

Ingredients

- 2-3 tbsp vegetable oil
- 1 onion , chopped
- 500g lamb mince
- 2 garlic cloves , finely chopped
- 2 tbsp curry powder
- 1 large sweet potato (about 300g), peeled and grated
- 100g frozen peas
- handful coriander , roughly chopped
- juice 0.5 lemon
- 3-4 sheets filo pastry
- 1 tsp cumin seeds

Method

STEP 1

Heat oven to 180C/160C fan/gas 4. Heat 1 tbsp of the oil in a frying pan. Cook the onion and mince for about 5 mins until the meat is browned. Stir in the garlic, curry powder, sweet potato and 300ml water. Cook for 5-8 mins until the potato has softened. Stir in the peas, coriander and a squeeze of lemon juice, then season.

STEP 2

Spoon the mixture into a baking dish. Brush the sheets of filo with the remaining oil and scrunch over the top of the mince. Sprinkle with cumin seeds and bake for 10-15 mins or until the top is crisp.

Red pepper & bean tikka masala

Prep:10 mins **Cook:**20 mins

Serves 2

Ingredients

- 1 tbsp vegetable oil
- 1 onion , chopped
- 2 red peppers , deseeded and cut into strips
- 1 garlic clove , crushed
- thumb-sized piece of ginger , grated
- 1 red chilli , finely chopped

- ½ tbsp garam masala
- ½ tbsp curry powder
- 1 tbsp tomato purée
- 415g can baked beans
- ½ lemon , juiced
- rice and coriander, to serve

Method

STEP 1

Heat the oil in a saucepan over a medium heat, add the onion and red peppers with a pinch of salt and fry until softened, around 5 mins. Tip in the garlic, ginger and red chilli along with the spices and fry for a couple of mins longer.

STEP 2

Spoon in the tomato purée, stir, then tip in the baked beans along with 100ml water. Bubble for 5 mins, then squeeze in the lemon juice. Serve with the rice and scatter over the coriander leaves.

Spicy chicken & bean stew

Prep: 15 mins **Cook:** 1 hr and 20 mins

Serves 6

Ingredients

- 1¼ kg chicken thighs and drumsticks (approx. weight, we used a 1.23kg mixed pack)
- 1 tbsp olive oil
- 2 onions, sliced
- 1 garlic clove, crushed
- 2 red chillies, deseeded and chopped
- 250g frozen peppers, defrosted
- 400g can chopped tomatoes
- 420g can kidney beans in chilli sauce
- 2 x 400g cans butter beans, drained
- 400ml hot chicken stock
- small bunch coriander, chopped
- 150ml pot soured cream and crusty bread, to serve

Method

STEP 1

Pull the skin off the chicken and discard. Heat the oil in a large casserole dish, brown the chicken all over, then remove with a slotted spoon. Tip in the onions, garlic and chillies, then fry for 5 mins until starting to soften and turn golden.

STEP 2

Add the peppers, tomatoes, beans and hot stock. Put the chicken back on top, half-cover with a pan lid and cook for 50 mins, until the chicken is cooked through and tender.

STEP 3

Stir through the coriander and serve with soured cream and crusty bread.

Lentil & cauliflower curry

Prep:10 mins **Cook:**40 mins

Serves 4

Ingredients

- 1 tbsp olive oil
- 1 large onion, chopped
- 3 tbsp curry paste
- 1 tsp turmeric
- 1 tsp mustard seeds
- 200g red or yellow lentil
- 1l low-sodium vegetable or chicken stock (made with 2 cubes)
- 1 large cauliflower, broken into florets
- 1 large potato, diced
- 3 tbsp coconut yogurt
- small pack coriander, chopped
- juice 1 lemon
- 100g cooked brown rice

Method

STEP 1

Heat the oil in a large saucepan and cook the onion until soft, about 5 mins. Add the curry paste, spices and lentils, then stir to coat the lentils in the onions and paste. Pour over the stock and simmer for 20 mins, then add the cauliflower, potato and a little extra water if it looks a bit dry.

STEP 2

Simmer for about 12 mins until the cauliflower and potatoes are tender. Stir in the yogurt, coriander and lemon juice, and serve with the brown rice.

Mushroom baked eggs with squished tomatoes

Prep:5 mins **Cook:**30 mins

Serves 2

Ingredients

- 2 large flat mushrooms (about 85g each), stalks removed and chopped
- rapeseed oil , for brushing
- ½ garlic clove , grated (optional)
- a few thyme leaves
- 2 tomatoes , halved
- 2 large eggs
- 2 handfuls rocket

Method

STEP 1

Heat oven to 200C/180C fan/gas 6. Brush the mushrooms with a little oil and the garlic (if using). Place the mushrooms in two very lightly greased gratin dishes, bottom-side up, and season lightly with pepper. Top with the chopped stalks and thyme, cover with foil and bake for 20 mins.

STEP 2

Remove the foil, add the tomatoes to the dishes and break an egg carefully onto each of the mushrooms. Season and add a little more thyme, if you like. Return to the oven for 10-12 mins or until the eggs are set but the yolks are still runny. Top with the rocket and eat straight from the dishes.

Crispy cod fingers with wedges & dill slaw

Prep:30 mins **Cook:**40 mins

Serves 4

Ingredients

- 3 large sweet potatoes (700g), scrubbed and cut into wedges
- ½ tbsp sunflower oil , plus a little extra
- ¼ large red cabbage
- ½ medium red onion , finely sliced

- 6 large cornichons , quartered
- 3 tbsp Greek yogurt or mayonnaise
- 25g dill , finely chopped
- 4 skinned cod fillets (160g per fillet)
- 2 large eggs
- 100g fresh breadcrumbs

Method

STEP 1

Heat oven to 200C/180C fan/gas 6. In a bowl, toss the wedges with the oil, 1 tsp salt and 1/4 tsp pepper. Transfer to a baking sheet and roast for 25-30 mins, turning halfway through. The wedges should be crisp and golden brown.

STEP 2

Meanwhile, make the slaw. Remove the cabbage's white core and discard. Slice the leaves as finely as possible and put in a large mixing bowl with the onion and cornichons. In another bowl, combine the yogurt or mayonnaise with the dill and 2 tbsp of the cornichons' pickling liquid. Mix the dressing with the other slaw ingredients until everything is well coated, then set aside.

STEP 3

Heat grill to high. Slice each cod fillet into two or three fingers. Beat the eggs lightly in a shallow bowl and tip the breadcrumbs into a separate bowl with a good pinch of salt and pepper. Dip each cod finger in the egg and then in the breadcrumbs, and place on an oiled baking sheet. Grill for 6-7 mins or until cooked through and golden. Serve with the crispy wedges and a generous helping of the dill pickle slaw.

Sunshine smoothie

Prep:5 mins no cook

Serves 3

Ingredients

- 500ml carrot juice, chilled
- 200g pineapple (fresh or canned)
- 2 bananas, broken into chunks
- small piece ginger, peeled
- 20g cashew nuts
- juice 1 lime

Method

STEP 1

Put the ingredients in a blender and whizz until smooth. Drink straight away or pour into a bottle to drink on the go. *Will keep in the fridge for a day.*

Caramelised onion & goat's cheese pizza

Prep:20 mins **Cook:**30 mins

Serves 2

Ingredients

For the base

- 125g wholemeal flour , plus a little for kneading if necessary
- ½ tsp instant yeast
- pinch of salt
- 1 tsp rapeseed oil , plus extra for greasing

For the topping

- 2 onions , halved and thinly sliced
- 2 tsp rapeseed oil
- 2 tsp balsamic vinegar
- 160g baby spinach leaves (not the very tiny ones), chopped
- 2 large garlic cloves , finely grated
- 50g soft goat's cheese
- 4 pitted Kalamata olives , quartered
- few soft thyme leaves
- 1 tsp sunflower seeds

Method

STEP 1

Heat oven to 220C/200C fan/gas 7. Tip the flour into a mixer with a dough hook, or a bowl. Add the yeast, salt, oil and just under 100ml warm water then mix to a soft dough. Knead in the food mixer for about 5 mins, but if making this by hand, tip onto a work surface and knead for about 10 mins. The dough is sticky, but try not to add too much extra flour. Leave in the bowl and cover with a tea towel while you make the topping. *There is no need to let the dough prove for a specific time – just let it sit while you get on with the next step.*

STEP 2

Tip the onions into a non-stick wok and add the oil, 4 tbsp water and balsamic vinegar. Cover with a saucepan lid that sits inside the pan to help the onions soften, then cook for 15 mins, stirring about 3 times and replacing the lid quickly so as not to lose too much moisture. After the time is up, the onions should be golden and all the liquid gone. Tip onto a plate. Add the spinach and garlic to the pan and stir-fry until the spinach has wilted.

STEP 3

Take the dough from the bowl and cut in half with an oiled knife, then press each piece into a 25-15 cm oval on a large greased baking sheet with oiled hands. Don't knead the dough first otherwise it will be too elastic and it will keep shrinking back.

STEP 4

Spread with the spinach followed by the onions, then dot with the cheese and scatter with the olives, thyme and sunflower seeds. Bake for 15 mins until golden and the base is cooked through.

Beef goulash soup

Prep:15 mins **Cook:**1 hr

Serves 2 - 3

Ingredients

- 1 tbsp rapeseed oil
- 1 large onion, halved and sliced
- 3 garlic cloves, sliced
- 200g extra lean stewing beef, finely diced
- 1 tsp caraway seeds
- 2 tsp smoked paprika
- 400g can chopped tomatoes
- 600ml beef stock
- 1 medium sweet potato, peeled and diced
- 1 green pepper, deseeded and diced

Supercharged topping

- 150g pot natural bio yogurt
- good handful parsley, chopped

Method

STEP 1

Heat the oil in a large pan, add the onion and garlic, and fry for 5 mins until starting to colour. Stir in the beef, increase the heat and fry, stirring, to brown it.

STEP 2

Add the caraway and paprika, stir well, then tip in the tomatoes and stock. Cover and leave to cook gently for 30 mins.

STEP 3

Stir in the sweet potato and green pepper, cover and cook for 20 mins more or until tender. Allow to cool a little, then serve topped with the yogurt and parsley (if the soup is too hot, it will kill the beneficial bacteria in the yogurt).

Prawn jalfrezi

Prep:10 mins **Cook:**22 mins

Serves 2

Ingredients

- 2 tsp rapeseed oil
- 2 medium onions , chopped
- thumb-sized piece ginger , finely chopped
- 2 garlic cloves , chopped
- 1 tsp ground coriander
- ½ tsp ground turmeric
- ½ tsp ground cumin
- ¼ tsp chilli flakes (or less if you don't like it too spicy)
- 400g can chopped tomato
- squeeze of clear honey
- 1 large green pepper , halved, deseeded and chopped
- small bunch coriander , stalks and leaves separated, chopped
- 140g large cooked peeled tiger prawns
- 250g pouch cooked brown rice
- minty yogurt or chutney, to serve (optional)

Method

STEP 1

Heat the oil in a non-stick pan and fry the onions, ginger and garlic for 8-10 mins, stirring frequently, until softened and starting to colour. Add the spices and chilli flakes, stir briefly, then pour in the tomatoes with half a can of water and the honey. Blitz everything in the pan with a hand blender until almost smooth (or use a food processor). Stir in the pepper and coriander stalks, cover the pan and leave to simmer for 10 mins. (The mixture will be very thick and splutter a little, so stir frequently.)

STEP 2

Stir in the prawns and scatter over the coriander leaves. Heat the rice following pack instructions. Serve both with a minty yogurt or chutney, if you like.

Vegan chocolate banana ice cream

Prep:5 mins **Serves 1**

Ingredients

- 1 frozen banana
- 1 tsp cocoa powder

Method

STEP 1

In a blender, blitz the frozen banana with the cocoa powder until smooth. Eat straight away.

Lighter South Indian fish curry

Prep:20 mins **Cook:**20 mins

Serves 4

Ingredients

- 1 tbsp rapeseed oil
- ½ tsp cumin seeds
- 1 medium onion , halved lengthways and thinly sliced into wedges
- 3 garlic cloves , finely chopped
- 1 tbsp finely chopped ginger (about a 2.5cm/1in piece)
- 12 dried curry leaves
- 1 tsp black mustard seeds
- 2 small green chillies , halved lengthways, deseeded (or leave a few seeds in if you want a bit of heat)
- 1 tsp ground coriander
- ½ tsp garam masala
- ¼ tsp turmeric
- 400g can reduced-fat coconut milk
- ¼ tsp ground black pepper

- 500g skinned, firm white fish fillets, such as cod or haddock
- 100g fine green beans , trimmed and halved lengthways
- 1 ripe mango
- generous handful roughly chopped coriander , leaves only
- 200g basmati rice , cooked, to serve
- lime wedges, to serve

Method

STEP 1

Heat the oil in a large non-stick frying or sauté pan. Add the cumin seeds and fry for 1 min, then tip in the onion, garlic and ginger, and fry for 1 min more. Stir in the curry leaves and mustard seeds, and fry about 3-4 mins on a medium heat, stirring occasionally, until the onions are turning brown. Stir in the chillies, coriander, garam masala and turmeric, and fry for 30 secs.

STEP 2

Stir the coconut milk in the can, then pour half into the pan. It should start to bubble and thicken, so let it simmer until quite thick, about 3 mins, stirring occasionally. Pour in the rest of the coconut milk, add the pepper and a pinch of salt, and lower the heat.

STEP 3

Sit the fish in the coconut milk and press it down to half submerge it. Cover the pan and simmer gently for 4-5 mins (depending on the thickness of your fillets) until the fish is almost cooked. Do not stir or the fish will break up – just spoon some of the sauce over the top of the fish halfway through, then remove the pan from the heat and let the fish sit for another 3-4 mins to finish cooking slowly. When done, it should feel firm and no longer be opaque. If you want a thinner sauce, pour in a spoonful or two of water.

STEP 4

Meanwhile, steam the green beans for about 4 mins until just tender. De-stone the mango and slice the flesh into thin wedges (see tip below left), then scatter over the fish to warm through.

STEP 5

To serve, break the fish into big chunks by removing it to serving bowls with a slotted spoon, then pour the sauce over and around it. Serve with the beans, a scattering of coriander and the rice, with lime wedges on the side to squeeze over.

Mexican chicken stew

Prep:20 mins **Cook:**25 mins

Serves 4

Ingredients

- 1 tbsp vegetable oil
- 1 medium onion, finely chopped
- 3 garlic cloves, finely chopped
- ½ tsp dark brown sugar
- 1 tsp chipotle paste (we used Discovery)
- 400g can chopped tomatoes
- 4 skinless, boneless chicken breasts
- 1 small red onion, sliced into rings
- a few coriander leaves
- corn tortillas, or rice to serve

Method

STEP 1

Heat the oil in a medium saucepan. Add the onion and cook for 5 mins or until softened and starting to turn golden, adding the garlic for the final min. Stir in the sugar, chipotle paste and tomatoes. Put the chicken into the pan, spoon over the sauce, and simmer gently for 20 mins until the chicken has cooked (add a splash of water if the sauce gets too dry).

STEP 2

Remove the chicken from the pan and shred with 2 forks, then stir back into the sauce. Scatter with a little red onion, the coriander, and serve with remaining red onion, tortillas or rice.

STEP 3

If you want to use a slow cooker, cook the onion and garlic as above, then put into your slow cooker with the sugar, chipotle, tomatoes and chicken. Cover and cook on High for 2 hours. Remove the chicken and shred then serve as above.

Healthy banana bread

Prep:20 mins **Cook:**1 hr and 15 mins

Cuts into 10 slices

Ingredients

- low-fat spread, for the tin, plus extra to serve
- 140g wholemeal flour
- 100g self-raising flour
- 1 tsp bicarbonate of soda

- 1 tsp baking powder
- 300g mashed banana from overripe black bananas
- 4 tbsp agave syrup
- 3 large eggs, beaten with a fork
- 150ml pot low-fat natural yogurt
- 25g chopped pecan or walnuts (optional)

Method

STEP 1

Heat oven to 160C/140C fan/gas 3. Grease and line a 2lb loaf tin with baking parchment (allow it to come 2cm above top of tin). Mix the flours, bicarb, baking powder and a pinch of salt in a large bowl.

STEP 2

Mix the bananas, syrup, eggs and yogurt. Quickly stir into dry ingredients, then gently scrape into the tin and scatter with nuts, if using. Bake for 1 hr 10 mins-1 hr 15 mins or until a skewer comes out clean.

STEP 3

Cool in tin on a wire rack. Eat warm or at room temperature, with low-fat spread.

Broccoli and kale green soup

Prep:15 mins **Cook:**20 mins

Serves 2

Ingredients

- 500ml stock , made by mixing 1 tbsp bouillon powder and boiling water in a jug
- 1 tbsp sunflower oil
- 2 garlic cloves , sliced
- thumb-sized piece ginger , sliced
- ½ tsp ground coriander
- 3cm/1in piece fresh turmeric root, peeled and grated, or 1/2 tsp ground turmeric
- pinch of pink Himalayan salt
- 200g courgettes , roughly sliced
- 85g broccoli
- 100g kale , chopped
- 1 lime , zested and juiced
- small pack parsley , roughly chopped, reserving a few whole leaves to serve

Method

STEP 1

Put the oil in a deep pan, add the garlic, ginger, coriander, turmeric and salt, fry on a medium heat for 2 mins, then add 3 tbsp water to give a bit more moisture to the spices.

STEP 2

Add the courgettes, making sure you mix well to coat the slices in all the spices, and continue cooking for 3 mins. Add 400ml stock and leave to simmer for 3 mins.

STEP 3

Add the broccoli, kale and lime juice with the rest of the stock. Leave to cook again for another 3-4 mins until all the vegetables are soft.

STEP 4

Take off the heat and add the chopped parsley. Pour everything into a blender and blend on high speed until smooth. It will be a beautiful green with bits of dark speckled through (which is the kale). Garnish with lime zest and parsley.

Easy creamy coleslaw

Prep:20 mins No cook

Serves 4

Ingredients

- ½ white cabbage , shredded
- 2 carrots , grated
- 4 spring onions , chopped
- 2 tbsp sultanas
- 3 tbsp low-fat mayonnaise
- 1 tbsp wholegrain mustard

Method

STEP 1

Put the cabbage, carrots, spring onions and sultanas in a large bowl and stir to combine.

STEP 2

Mix the mayonnaise with the mustard in another small bowl and drizzle over the veg. Fold everything together to coat in the creamy sauce, then season to taste.

Spicy spaghetti with garlic mushrooms

Prep:10 mins **Cook:**15 mins

Serves 4

Ingredients

- 2 tbsp olive oil
- 250g pack chestnut mushroom, thickly sliced
- 1 garlic clove, thinly sliced
- small bunch parsley, leaves only
- 1 celery stick, finely chopped
- 1 onion, finely chopped
- 400g can chopped tomato
- 1/2 red chilli, deseeded and finely chopped, (or use drieds chilli flakes)
- 300g spaghetti

Method

STEP 1

Heat 1 tbsp oil in a pan, add the mushrooms, then fry over a high heat for 3 mins until golden and softened. Add the garlic, fry for 1 min more, then tip into a bowl with the parsley. Add the onion and celery to the pan with the rest of the oil, then fry for 5 mins until lightly coloured.

STEP 2

Stir in the tomatoes, chilli and a little salt, then bring to the boil. Reduce the heat and simmer, uncovered, for 10 mins until thickened. Meanwhile, boil the spaghetti, then drain. Toss with the sauce, top with the garlicky mushrooms, then serve.

Berry Bircher

Prep:5 mins plus overnight chilling, no cook

Serves 2

Ingredients

- 70g porridge oats
- 2 tbsp golden linseeds
- 2 ripe bananas
- 140g frozen raspberries

- 175g natural bio yogurt

Method

STEP 1

Tip the oats and seeds into a bowl, and pour over 200ml boiling water and stir well. Add the bananas and three-quarters of the raspberries (chill the remainder), mash together, then cover and chill overnight.

STEP 2

The next day, layer the raspberry oats in two tumblers or bowls with the yogurt, top with the reserved raspberries and serve.

Spinach & chickpea curry

Prep:5 mins **Cook:**15 mins

Serves 4

Ingredients

- 2 tbsp mild curry paste
- 1 onion, chopped
- 400g can cherry tomatoes
- 2 x 400g cans chickpeas, drained and rinsed
- 250g bag baby leaf spinach
- squeeze lemon juice
- basmati rice, to serve

Method

STEP 1

Heat the curry paste in a large non-stick frying pan. Once it starts to split, add the onion and cook for 2 mins to soften. Tip in the tomatoes and bubble for 5 mins or until the sauce has reduced.

STEP 2

Add the chickpeas and some seasoning, then cook for 1 min more. Take off the heat, then tip in the spinach and allow the heat of the pan to wilt the leaves. Season, add the lemon juice, and serve with basmati rice.

Sweet potato & sprout hash with poached eggs

Prep:15 mins **Cook:**25 mins

Serves 3

Ingredients

- 2 large sweet potatoes , cut into chunks
- 2 tsp olive oil
- 2 red onions , thinly sliced
- 300g Brussels sprouts , thinly sliced
- grating of nutmeg
- 3 eggs

Method

STEP 1

Put the sweet potatoes in a bowl, cover with cling film and microwave on high for 5 mins until tender but still holding their shape. Uncover the bowl and leave to cool a little.

STEP 2

Meanwhile, heat the oil in a wide non-stick frying pan and add the onions. Cook for 5-8 mins until starting to caramelise. Add the sprouts and stir-fry over a high heat until softened. Push the sprouts and onions to one side of the pan and add the sweet potatoes, squashing them down in the pan with the back of a spatula. Leave undisturbed for 5 mins until starting to crisp on the underside. Season, add the nutmeg, mix in the sprouts and onions, and flip the potato over, trying not to break it up too much. Cook for a further 5 mins until really crispy.

STEP 3

Meanwhile, poach 3 eggs in a pan of barely simmering water. Serve the hash topped with poached eggs.

Spiced mushroom & lentil hotpot

Prep:10 mins **Cook:**35 mins

Serves 4

Ingredients

- 2 tbsp olive oil
- 1 medium onion, sliced
- 300g mini Portobello mushrooms or chestnut mushrooms, sliced
- 2 garlic cloves, crushed
- 1 ½ tsp ground cumin
- 1 tsp smoked paprika

- 2 x 400g cans green lentils, drained and rinsed (drained weight 240g)
- 1 tbsp soy sauce
- 1 tbsp balsamic vinegar
- 1 medium sweet potato, peeled and very thinly sliced
- 1 large potato, very thinly sliced
- 1 thyme sprig, leaves picked

Method

STEP 1

Heat oven to 200C/180C fan/gas 6. Heat half the oil in a medium saucepan. Fry the onion for 3 mins, then add the mushrooms. Cook for another 3 mins, then increase the heat and add the garlic, ground cumin and paprika, and cook for 1 min. Remove from the heat and add the lentils, soy sauce, balsamic vinegar and 100ml water. Season, then tip the mixture into a casserole dish.

STEP 2

Rinse the saucepan and return to the hob. Add a kettle full of boiled water and bring back to the boil over a high heat. Add the potato slices, cook for 3 mins, then drain. Arrange on top of the lentils, then brush with the remaining oil. Roast in the oven for 25 mins until the potatoes are golden, then scatter over the thyme before serving.

Mexican bean soup with crispy feta tortillas

Prep:10 mins **Cook:**15 mins

Serves 4

Ingredients

- 1 tbsp vegetable oil
- 1 onion , chopped
- 1 heaped tbsp chipotle paste
- 500g carton passata
- 500ml vegetable stock
- 400g can kidney beans , drained and rinsed
- 400g can black beans , drained and rinsed
- 200g feta
- 2 garlic cloves , crushed
- 4 large or 8 small flour tortillas
- small pack coriander , roughly chopped, to serve

Method

STEP 1

Heat the oil in a large pan and cook the onion over a medium heat for 10 mins to soften. Stir in the chipotle paste, passata, stock and all the beans. Season, bring to the boil, then gently simmer for 5 mins.

STEP 2

Meanwhile, in a bowl crumble the feta and mix with the garlic. Divide between the tortillas, spreading over one half of each, then sprinkle over a little pepper. Fold the uncovered side over and press down. Heat a dry frying pan and cook the tortillas on both sides for a couple of mins until the feta has melted and the tortillas are crisp.

STEP 3

Divide the soup between bowls, scatter with coriander and serve with the tortillas.

Rosemary chicken with oven-roasted ratatouille

Prep:15 mins **Cook:**40 mins

Serves 4

Ingredients

- 1 aubergine , cut into chunky pieces
- 2 courgettes , sliced into half-moons
- 3 mixed peppers , deseeded and roughly chopped
- 2 tsp finely chopped rosemary , plus 4 small sprigs
- 2 large garlic cloves , crushed
- 3 tbsp olive oil
- 4 skinless, boneless chicken breasts
- 250g cherry or baby plum tomato , halved

Method

STEP 1

Heat oven to 200C/180C fan/gas 6. In a large roasting tin, toss together the aubergine, courgettes and peppers with half the chopped rosemary, half the garlic, 2 tbsp oil and some seasoning. Spread out the vegetables in an even layer, then roast in the oven for 20 mins.

STEP 2

Meanwhile, mix remaining rosemary, garlic and oil together. Slash each of the chicken breasts 4-5 times with a sharp knife, brush over the flavoured oil, season and chill for 15 mins.

STEP 3

After veg have cooked for 20 mins, stir in the tomatoes. Make spaces in the roasting tin and nestle the chicken breasts amongst the vegetables. Place a rosemary sprig on top of each chicken breast. Return the tin to the oven for 18-20 mins, until the chicken is cooked through and the vegetables are lightly caramelised. Serve with some new potatoes, if you like.

Moroccan chicken with sweet potato mash

Prep: 10 mins **Cook:** 25 mins

Serves 4

Ingredients

- 1kg sweet potatoes , cubed
- 2 tsp ras-el-hanout , or a mix of ground cinnamon and cumin
- 4 skinless, boneless chicken breasts
- 2 tbsp olive oil
- 1 onion , thinly sliced
- 1 fat garlic clove , crushed
- 200ml chicken stock
- 2 tsp clear honey
- juice ½ lemon
- handful green olives , pitted or whole
- 20g pack coriander , leaves chopped

Method

STEP 1

Boil the potatoes in salted water for 15 mins or until tender. Mix the ras el hanout with seasoning, then sprinkle all over the chicken. Heat 1 tbsp oil in large frying pan, then brown the chicken for 3 mins on each side until golden.

STEP 2

Lift the chicken out of the pan. Add the onion and garlic and cook for 5 mins until softened. Add the stock, honey, lemon juice and olives, return the chicken to the pan, then simmer for 10 mins until the sauce is syrupy and the chicken cooked.

STEP 3

Mash the potatoes with 1 tbsp oil and season. Thickly slice each chicken breast and stir the coriander through the sauce. Serve the chicken and sauce over mash.

Butternut & cinnamon oats

Prep:10 mins **Cook:**10 mins plus overnight soaking

Serves 4

Ingredients

- 120g porridge oats
- 80g raisins
- 2 tsp ground cinnamon , plus a sprinkling to serve
- large chunk butternut squash , peeled and coarsely grated (approx 320g grated weight)
- 2 x 150ml pots bio yogurt
- 25g walnuts roughly broken
- milk , to serve (optional)

Method

STEP 1

Tip the oats, raisins and cinnamon into a large bowl and pour over 1 litre cold water. Cover the bowl and leave to soak overnight.

STEP 2

The next morning, tip the contents into a large saucepan and stir in the grated squash. Cook for about 8-10 mins over a medium heat, stirring frequently, until the oats are cooked and the squash is soft. Add a little more water if it's too thick.

STEP 3

Put half of the mixture in the fridge for the next day. Spoon the remainder into bowls, top each portion with 1 pot yogurt and half the nuts. Dust with cinnamon, then serve with a splash of milk.

Pizza sauce

Prep:5 mins **Cook:**50 mins

makes 4-6 pizzas

Ingredients

- 2 tbsp olive oil
- 1 small onion, finely chopped
- 1 fat garlic clove, crushed

- 2 x 400g cans chopped tomatoes
- 3 tbsp tomato purée
- 1 bay leaf
- 2 tbsp dried oregano
- 2 tsp brown sugar
- 1 small bunch basil, finely chopped

Method

STEP 1

Heat the oil in a saucepan over a low heat, then add the onion along with a generous pinch of salt. Fry gently for 12-15 mins or until the onion has softened and is turning translucent. Add the garlic and fry for a further min. Tip in the tomatoes and purée along with the bay, oregano and sugar. Bring to the boil and lower the heat. Simmer, uncovered, for 30-35 mins or until thickened and reduced. Season. For a really smooth sauce, blitz with a stick blender, otherwise leave as is.

STEP 2

Stir the basil into the sauce. The sauce will cover 4-6 large pizza bases. *Keeps well in the fridge for 1 week or stored in a container in the freezer.*

Ultimate veggie burger with pickled carrot slaw

Prep:15 mins **Cook:**20 mins plus chilling

Serves 4

Ingredients

- 2 tsp vegetable oil , plus extra for frying
- 1 small onion , diced
- 2 garlic cloves , chopped
- 2 large Portobello mushrooms , finely chopped
- 2 small sweet potatoes , peeled and diced
- 150g cooked quinoa
- 1 large beetroot , grated
- 1 egg , beaten
- 2 tbsp chopped coriander
- zest 2 limes
- 4 tbsp plain flour , plus extra for dusting

For the carrot slaw

- 1 large carrot , thinly shredded
- 2 tbsp rice wine vinegar
- 1 tsp golden caster sugar

To serve

- 2 tbsp mayonnaise
- 1 tbsp chilli sauce
- 4 burger buns , lightly toasted
- 2 handfuls rocket or spinach leaves

Method

STEP 1

In a medium frying pan, heat 2 tsp vegetable oil. Add the onion, garlic and mushrooms, season and fry until everything is soft, about 5 mins. Put the sweet potatoes in a microwaveable bowl, cover with cling film and microwave on high for 5-6 mins until soft. Mash the sweet potatoes, then add to the pan with the onion mix. Tip into a large mixing bowl and leave to cool.

STEP 2

Add the quinoa, beetroot, egg, coriander, lime zest, flour and some seasoning. Mix with your hands, then form into four large burgers. Sprinkle with flour and chill for 30 mins to firm up.

STEP 3

Put the carrots in a small bowl with the vinegar, sugar and 1 tsp salt. Cover and leave to pickle until ready to eat. Mix the mayonnaise with the chilli sauce.

STEP 4

Heat a frying pan and pour in a thin coating of oil. Fry the burgers on a medium-low heat to allow the centre to cook slowly. When browned, after about 7 mins, gently flip over and cook for the same time on the other side. Drain the pickled carrots and toast the buns.

STEP 5

Brush the buns with the chilli mayo. Layer on the spinach or rocket, burgers and the carrot slaw.

Gnocchi with roasted red pepper sauce

Prep:2 mins **Cook:**25 mins

Serves 4

Ingredients

- 500g pack gnocchi
- ½ batch roasted red pepper sauce (see 'Goes well with…' below)
- 125g ball mozzarella
- 2 handfuls breadcrumbs

Method

STEP 1

Heat the oven to 180C/ 160C fan/ gas 4. Cook a 500g pack gnocchi following pack instructions, then drain and tip into a casserole dish. Pour over ½ batch roasted red pepper sauce (see 'Goes well with…' below), then tear 125g ball mozzarella over the top and sprinkle over 2 handfuls breadcrumbs. Bake for 20 mins until golden and heated through.

Speedy Mediterranean gnocchi

Cook:5 mins **Serves 2**

Ingredients

- 400g gnocchi
- 200g chargrilled vegetables (from the deli counter - I used chargrilled peppers, aubergines, artichokes and semi-dried tomatoes)
- 2 tbsp red pesto
- a handful of basil leaves
- parmesan or pecorino (or vegetarian alternative), to serve

Method

STEP 1

Boil a large pan of salted water. Add the gnocchi, cook for 2 mins or until it rises to the surface, then drain and tip back into the pan with a splash of reserved cooking water.

STEP 2

Add the chargrilled veg, chopped into pieces if large, red pesto and basil leaves. Serve with shavings of Parmesan or pecorino (or vegetarian alternative).

Creamy tomato, courgette & prawn pasta

Prep:10 mins **Cook:**25 mins

Serves 4

Ingredients

- 1 tbsp olive oil
- 2 fat garlic cloves , thinly sliced
- 2 large or 400g baby courgettes , sliced
- 400g orecchiette pasta, or any other small pasta shape
- 2 x 400g cans cherry tomatoes
- good pinch of sugar
- 200g raw prawn , peeled
- 100g half-fat crème fraîche
- small pack basil , leaves only, torn

Method

STEP 1

Heat the oil in a large pan, add the garlic and sizzle for a few mins, then add the courgettes and cook for a few mins more until starting to soften. Cook the pasta following pack instructions.

STEP 2

Add the tomatoes, sugar and seasoning to the pan, stir and simmer, uncovered, for about 10 mins while the pasta cooks.

STEP 3

Add the prawns to the sauce and bubble until they just turn pink. Drain the pasta and add to the sauce with the crème fraîche. Simmer for another 1-2 mins, then add the basil and serve.

Spelt & wild mushroom risotto

Prep:15 mins **Cook:**35 mins Plus 20 mins soaking

Serves 4

Ingredients

- 200g pearled spelt
- 25g dried porcini mushrooms
- ½ tbsp olive oil
- 1 onion , finely diced
- 2 garlic cloves , finely chopped
- 100g chestnut button mushroom , cut into quarters
- 100ml white wine
- 1l hot vegetable stock

- 1 tbsp low-fat crème fraîche
- bunch chives , finely chopped
- handful grated pecorino or parmesan to serve (optional)

Method

STEP 1

Cover the spelt with cold water and soak the dried mushrooms in 100ml boiling water in a separate bowl for 20 mins. Heat the olive oil in a large frying pan. Tip in the onion and garlic, cook for 2 mins, then add the chestnut mushrooms and cook for a further 2 mins. Drain the spelt and add along with the wine. Simmer until almost all the liquid evaporates, stirring often.

STEP 2

Drain the porcini mushrooms, add them to the pan and the soaking liquid to the vegetable stock. Stir in the stock 1 cup at a time and simmer, stirring often, until all liquid is absorbed and the spelt is just tender, about 20 mins in total. Stir in the crème fraîche and season with salt and pepper. Spoon onto plates and sprinkle over chives and cheese (if using).

Chickpea & coriander burgers

Prep:15 mins **Cook:**10 mins Plus chilling

Serves 4

Ingredients

- 400g can chickpeas, drained
- zest 1 lemon, plus juice ½
- 1 tsp ground cumin
- small bunch coriander, chopped
- 1 egg
- 100g fresh breadcrumbs
- 1 medium red onion, ½ diced, ½ sliced
- 1 tbsp olive oil
- 4 small wholemeal buns
- 1 large tomato, sliced, ½ cucumber, sliced and chilli sauce, to serve

Method

STEP 1

In a food processor, whizz the chickpeas, lemon zest, lemon juice, cumin, half the coriander, the egg and some seasoning. Scrape into a bowl and mix with 80g of the breadcrumbs and the diced onions. Form 4 burgers, press remaining breadcrumbs onto both sides and chill for at least 10 mins.

STEP 2

Heat the oil in a frying pan until hot. Fry the burgers for 4 mins each side, keeping the heat on medium so they don't burn. To serve, slice each bun and fill with a slice of tomato, a burger, a few red onion slices, some cucumber slices, a dollop of chilli sauce and the remaining coriander.

Korean clam broth - Jogaetang

Prep: 10 mins **Cook:** 10 mins

Serves 4

Ingredients

- 500g medium-sized clams , rinsed (see below)
- 1 tbsp gochujang chilli paste or white miso if you don't want it to be spicy
- 2 large garlic cloves , finely chopped
- 3 spring onions , whites finely sliced, greens roughly chopped
- 2 handfuls beansprouts
- 1 green chilli , cut into matchsticks
- toasted sesame oil , to serve
- cooked rice , to serve
- kimchi or pickled cucumber, to serve

Method

STEP 1

Drain the rinsed clams well and place them in a saucepan (with a lid) that fits them in a single layer. Pour over cold water to just cover (about 750ml should do it), then stir in the chilli paste, the garlic and the spring onion whites.

STEP 2

Cover with a lid, bring to the boil, then turn down the heat and simmer gently for 2-3 mins until the clams have all opened. Turn off the heat and stir through the beansprouts and chilli. Season with salt to taste, and decant into one large or two smaller bowls. Top with the spring onion greens and a drizzle of sesame oil, and enjoy with rice and something sharp like kimchi or pickled cucumber. You'll need soup spoons and a bowl for the empty shells.

Cajun prawn pizza

Prep:10 mins **Cook:**20 mins

Serves 2

Ingredients

For the base

- 200g wholemeal flour , plus a little for kneading if necessary
- 1 tsp instant yeast
- pinch of salt
- 2 tsp rapeseed oil , plus extra greasing

For the topping

- 1 tbsp rapeseed oil , plus extra for greasing
- 2 large sticks celery , finely chopped
- 1 yellow pepper or green pepper, de-seeded and diced
- 225g can chopped tomatoes
- 1 tsp smoked paprika
- 165g pack raw, peeled king prawns
- 2-3 tbsp chopped coriander
- ½ - 1 tsp Cajun spice mix
- 2 handfuls rocket , optional

Method

STEP 1

Heat oven to 220C/200C fan/gas 7. Tip the flour into a mixer with a dough hook, or a bowl. Add the yeast, salt, oil and 150ml warm water then mix well to a soft dough. Knead in the food mixer for about 5 mins, but if making this by hand, tip onto a work surface and knead for about 10 mins. The dough is sticky, but try not to add too much extra flour. Leave in the bowl and cover with a tea towel while you make the topping. *There is no need to prove the dough for a specific time, just let it sit while you get on with the next step.*

STEP 2

For the topping: heat the oil in a non-stick pan or wok. Add the celery and pepper and fry for 8 mins, stirring frequently, until softened. Tip in the tomatoes and paprika then cook for 2 mins more. Set aside to cool a little then stir in the prawns.

STEP 3

With an oiled knife, cut the dough in half and shape each piece into a 25cm round with lightly oiled hands on oiled baking sheets. Don't knead the dough first otherwise it will be too elastic and will shrink back. Spread each with half of the tomato and prawn mix then scatter with the coriander and sprinkle with the Cajun spice. Bake for 10 mins until golden. Serve with a green salad.

Rice pudding

Prep:5 mins **Cook:**2 hrs

Serves 4

Ingredients

- 100g pudding rice
- butter, for the dish
- 50g sugar
- 700ml semi-skimmed milk
- pinch of grated nutmeg or strip lemon zest
- 1 bay leaf, or strip lemon zest

Method

STEP 1

Heat the oven to 150C/130C fan/gas 2. Wash and drain the rice. Butter a 850ml baking dish, then tip in the rice and sugar and stir through the milk. Sprinkle in the nutmeg and top with the bay leaf or lemon zest.

STEP 2

Cook for 2 hrs or until the pudding wobbles ever so slightly when shaken.

Burnt aubergine veggie chilli

Prep:25 mins **Cook:**2 hrs

Serves 4

Ingredients

- 1 aubergine
- 1 tbsp olive oil or rapeseed oil
- 1 red onion, diced
- 2 carrots, finely diced
- 70g puy lentils or green lentils, rinsed
- 30g red lentils, rinsed

- 400g can kidney beans
- 3 tbsp dark soy sauce
- 400g can chopped tomatoes
- 20g dark chocolate, finely chopped
- ¼ tsp chilli powder
- 2 tsp dried oregano
- 2 tsp ground cumin
- 2 tsp sweet smoked paprika
- 1 tsp coriander
- 1 tsp cinnamon
- 800ml vegetable stock
- ½ lime, juiced

To serve

- brown rice
- tortilla chips, mashed avocado, yogurt or soured cream, grated cheddar, roughly chopped coriander (optional)

Method

STEP 1

If you have a gas hob, put the aubergine directly onto a lit ring to char completely, turning occasionally with kitchen tongs, until burnt all over. Alternatively, use a barbecue or heat the grill to its highest setting and cook, turning occasionally, until completely blackened (the grill won't give you the same smoky flavour). Set aside to cool on a plate, then peel off the charred skin and remove the stem. Roughly chop the flesh and set aside.

STEP 2

In a large pan, heat the oil, add the onion and carrots with a pinch of salt, and fry over a low-medium heat for 15-20 mins until the carrots have softened.

STEP 3

Add the aubergine, both types of lentils, the kidney beans with the liquid from the can, soy sauce, tomatoes, chocolate, chilli powder, oregano and the spices. Stir to combine, then pour in the stock. Bring to the boil, then turn down the heat to very low. Cover with a lid and cook for 11/2 hrs, checking and stirring every 15-20 mins to prevent it from burning.

STEP 4

Remove the lid and let the mixture simmer over a low-medium heat, stirring occasionally, for about 15 mins until you get a thick sauce. Stir in the lime juice and taste for seasoning – add more salt if needed. Serve hot over rice with whichever accompaniments you want!

Spiced lentil & butternut squash soup

Prep:10 mins **Cook:**40 mins

Serves 4-6

Ingredients

- 2 tbsp olive oil
- 2 onions, finely chopped
- 2 garlic cloves, crushed
- ¼ tsp hot chilli powder
- 1 tbsp ras el hanout
- 1 butternut squash, peeled and cut into 2cm pieces
- 100g red lentils
- 1l hot vegetable stock
- 1 small bunch coriander, leaves chopped, plus extra to serve
- dukkah (see tip) and natural yogurt, to serve

Method

STEP 1

Heat the oil in a large flameproof casserole dish or saucepan over a medium-high heat. Fry the onions with a pinch of salt for 7 mins, or until softened and just caramelised. Add the garlic, chilli and ras el hanout, and cook for 1 min more.

STEP 2

Stir in the squash and lentils. Pour over the stock and season to taste. Bring to the boil, then reduce the heat to a simmer and cook, covered, for 25 mins or until the squash is soft. Blitz the soup with a stick blender until smooth, then season to taste. *To freeze, leave to cool completely and transfer to large freezerproof bags.*

STEP 3

Stir in the coriander leaves and ladle the soup into bowls. Serve topped with the dukkah, yogurt and extra coriander leaves.

Lentil soup

Prep:10 mins **Cook:**1 hr

Serves 4

Ingredients

- 2l vegetable or ham stock
- 150g red lentils
- 6 carrots, finely chopped
- 2 medium leeks, sliced (about 300g)
- small handful of chopped parsley, to serve

Method

STEP 1

Heat the stock in a large pan and add the lentils. Bring to the boil and allow the lentils to soften for a few minutes.

STEP 2

Add the carrots and leeks and season (don't add salt if you use ham stock as it will make it too salty). Bring to the boil, then reduce the heat, cover and simmer for 45-60 mins until the lentils have broken down. Scatter over the parsley and serve with buttered bread, if you like.

Tandoori chicken

Prep:30 mins **Cook:**15 mins

Serves 8

Ingredients

- juice 2 lemons
- 4 tsp paprika
- 2 red onions, finely chopped
- 16 skinless chicken thighs
- vegetable oil, for brushing
- For the marinade
- 300ml Greek yogurt
- large piece ginger, grated
- 4 garlic cloves, crushed
- ¾ tsp garam masala
- ¾ tsp ground cumin
- ½ tsp chilli powder

- ¼ tsp turmeric

Method

STEP 1

Mix the lemon juice with the paprika and red onions in a large shallow dish. Slash each chicken thigh three times, then turn them in the juice and set aside for 10 mins.

STEP 2

Mix all of the marinade ingredients together and pour over the chicken. Give everything a good mix, then cover and chill for at least 1 hr. This can be done up to a day in advance.

STEP 3

Heat the grill. Lift the chicken pieces onto a rack over a baking tray. Brush over a little oil and grill for 8 mins on each side or until lightly charred and completely cooked through.

Mexican penne with avocado

Prep:10 mins **Cook:**20 mins

Serves 2

Ingredients

- 100g wholemeal penne
- 1 tsp rapeseed oil
- 1 large onion, sliced, plus 1 tbsp finely chopped
- 1 orange pepper, deseeded and cut into chunks
- 2 garlic cloves, grated
- 2 tsp mild chilli powder
- 1 tsp ground coriander
- ½ tsp cumin seeds
- 400g can chopped tomatoes
- 196g can sweetcorn in water
- 1 tsp vegetable bouillon powder
- 1 avocado, stoned and chopped
- 1/2 lime, zest and juice
- handful coriander, chopped, plus extra to serve

Method

STEP 1

Cook the pasta in salted water for 10-12 mins until al dente. Meanwhile, heat the oil in a medium pan. Add the sliced onion and pepper and fry, stirring frequently for 10 mins until golden. Stir in the garlic and spices, then tip in the tomatoes, half a can of water, the corn and bouillon. Cover and simmer for 15 mins.

STEP 2

Meanwhile, toss the avocado with the lime juice and zest, and the finely chopped onion.

STEP 3

Drain the penne and toss into the sauce with the coriander. Spoon the pasta into bowls, top with the avocado and scatter over the coriander leaves.

Double bean & roasted pepper chilli

Prep:30 mins **Cook:**1 hr and 15 mins

Serves 8

Ingredients

- 2 onions, chopped
- 2 celery sticks, finely chopped
- 2 yellow or orange peppers, finely chopped
- 2 tbsp sunflower oil or rapeseed oil
- 2 x 460g jars roasted red peppers
- 2 tsp chipotle paste
- 2 tbsp red wine vinegar
- 1 tbsp cocoa powder
- 1 tbsp dried oregano
- 1 tbsp sweet smoked paprika
- 2 tbsp ground cumin
- 1 tsp ground cinnamon
- 2 x 400g cans chopped tomatoes
- 400g can refried beans
- 3 x 400g cans kidney beans, drained and rinsed
- 2 x 400g cans black beans, drained and rinsed

Method

STEP 1

Put the onions, celery and chopped peppers with the oil in your largest flameproof casserole dish or heavy-based saucepan, and fry gently over a low heat until soft but not coloured.

STEP 2

Drain both jars of peppers over a bowl to catch the juices. Put a quarter of the peppers into a food processor with the chipotle paste, vinegar, cocoa, dried spices and herbs. Whizz to a purée, then stir into the softened veg and cook for a few mins.

STEP 3

Add the tomatoes and refried beans with 1 can water and the reserved pepper juice. Simmer for 1 hr until thickened, smoky and the tomato chunks have broken down to a smoother sauce.

STEP 4

At this stage you can cool and chill the sauce if making ahead. Otherwise add the kidney and black beans, and the remaining roasted peppers, cut into bite-sized pieces, then reheat. (This makes a large batch, so once the sauce is ready it might be easier to split it between two pans when you add the beans and peppers.) Once bubbling and the beans are hot, season to taste and serve.

Slow-cooker chicken curry

Prep: 10 mins **Cook:** 6 hrs Plus overnight chilling

Serves 2

Ingredients

- 1 large onion, roughly chopped
- 3 tbsp mild curry paste
- 400g can chopped tomatoes
- 2 tsp vegetable bouillon powder
- 1 tbsp finely chopped ginger
- 1 yellow pepper, deseeded and chopped
- 2 skinless chicken legs, fat removed
- 30g pack fresh coriander, leaves chopped
- cooked brown rice, to serve

Method

STEP 1

Put 1 roughly chopped large onion, 3 tbsp mild curry paste, a 400g can chopped tomatoes, 2 tsp vegetable bouillon powder, 1 tbsp finely chopped ginger and 1 chopped yellow pepper into the slow cooker pot with a third of a can of water and stir well.

STEP 2

Add 2 skinless chicken legs, fat removed, and push them under all the other ingredients so that they are completely submerged. Cover with the lid and chill in the fridge overnight.

STEP 3

The next day, cook on Low for 6 hrs until the chicken and vegetables are really tender.

STEP 4

Stir in the the chopped leaves of 30g coriander just before serving over brown rice.

Vegetarian bolognese

Prep:10 mins **Cook:**1 hr

Serves 4

Ingredients

- 2 tbsp olive oil
- 1 medium onion , finely chopped
- 2 carrots , very finely chopped
- 2 celery sticks , very finely chopped
- 1 garlic clove , crushed
- 350g frozen Quorn mince
- 1 bay leaf
- 500ml passata
- 1 good-quality vegetable stock cube
- 100ml milk
- small bunch basil , chopped
- 600g cooked spaghetti or other pasta shape (about 250g dried)
- vegetarian hard cheese , to serve
- Method

STEP 1

Heat the oil in a saucepan and gently fry the onion, carrots and celery until the onion is starting to soften. Stir in the garlic and the Quorn (there's no need to defrost it) and fry for a couple of mins. Add the bay leaf, passata, vegetable stock cube and 200ml water, then bring everything to the boil.

STEP 2

Turn down the heat and simmer for 30 mins or until all the pieces of veg are tender and disappearing into the tomato sauce. Add the milk, then cover with a lid and cook for 10 mins. Season to taste. If the sauce is a bit thin, keep bubbling until it thickens. Stir through the basil. Serve with the spaghetti and grate the cheese over the top, if you like. *Can be frozen into portions and reheated.*

Quinoa chilli with avocado & coriander

Prep:10 mins **Cook:**45 mins

Serves 2

Ingredients

- 1 tbsp rapeseed oil
- 1 large onion , sliced
- 2 large garlic cloves , chopped
- 1 green pepper , chopped
- ½-1 tsp smoked paprika
- ½-1 tsp chilli powder
- 2 tsp cumin
- 2 tsp coriander
- 400g can chopped tomatoes
- ½ tsp dried oregano
- 2 tsp vegetable bouillon powder (check the label if you're vegan)
- 80g quinoa , rinsed under cold water
- 400g can black beans , drained and rinsed
- generous handful of coriander , chopped
- 2 tbsp bio yogurt or coconut yogurt (optional)
- 1 small avocado , stoned, peeled and sliced

Method

STEP 1

Heat the oil in a non-stick frying pan and fry the onion and garlic for 8 mins. Add the pepper and spices to taste and fry for 1 min more.

STEP 2

Tip in the tomatoes and a can of water, stir in the oregano, bouillon and quinoa, bring to the boil, then cover and simmer for 20 mins.

STEP 3

Stir in the black beans and cook, uncovered, for 5 mins more. Add most of the coriander, then serve topped with the yogurt (if using), the remaining coriander and the avocado slices.

Crispy chilli turkey noodles

Prep:5 mins **Cook:**15 mins

Serves 4

Ingredients

- 2 tbsp sesame oil
- 500g turkey mince
- 5cm piece ginger , grated
- 1 large garlic clove , crushed
- 3 tbsp honey
- 3 tbsp soy sauce
- 1 tbsp hot sriracha chilli sauce
- 350g dried udon noodles
- 2 limes , juiced, plus wedges to serve (optional)
- 2 large carrots , peeled and cut into matchsticks
- 4 spring onions , shredded
- 1 small bunch coriander , sliced (optional)

Method

STEP 1

Heat 1 tbsp oil in a large non-stick frying pan over a high heat. Once hot, add the turkey mince to the pan and fry for 10-12 mins until golden brown and crispy, breaking up the meat with a wooden spoon as you go. Add the ginger and garlic to the pan and cook for 1 min. Stir in the honey, soy and chilli sauce and cook for 2 mins.

STEP 2

Meanwhile, bring a large pan of water to the boil, add the noodles and cook following pack instructions. Drain and toss the noodles with the remaining 1 tbsp oil and all the lime juice, then divide between bowls. Top with the crispy turkey mince, carrot, onion and coriander. Serve with extra lime wedges for squeezing over, if you like.

Orzo & tomato soup

Prep:5 mins **Cook:**25 mins

Serves 4

Ingredients

- 2 tbsp olive oil
- 1 onion, chopped
- 2 celery sticks, chopped
- 2 garlic cloves, crushed
- 1 tbsp tomato purée
- 400g can chopped tomatoes
- 400g can chickpeas
- 150g orzo pasta
- 700ml vegetable stock
- 2 tbsp basil pesto
- crusty bread, to serve

Method

STEP 1

Heat 1 tbsp olive oil in a large saucepan. Add the onion and celery and fry for 10-15 mins, or until starting to soften, then add the garlic and cook for 1 min more. Stir in all the other ingredients, except for the pesto and remaining oil, and bring to the boil.

STEP 2

Reduce the heat and leave to simmer for 6-8 mins, or until the orzo is tender. Season to taste, then ladle into bowls.

STEP 3

Stir the remaining oil with the pesto, then drizzle over the soup. Serve with chunks of crusty bread.

Pasta arrabbiata with aubergine

Prep:8 mins **Cook:**35 mins

Serves 2

Ingredients

- 1 tbsp cold-pressed rapeseed oil
- 1 large onion , finely chopped (160g)
- 2 large garlic cloves , finely grated
- 1 tsp chilli flakes
- 1 tsp smoked paprika
- 400g can chopped tomatoes
- 1 tsp vegetable bouillon powder

- 1 aubergine , chopped
- 150g wholemeal penne or fusilli
- large handful of basil , plus extra to serve
- 25g parmesan or vegetarian Italian-style hard cheese, finely grated

Method

STEP 1

Heat the oil in a large non-stick pan, add the onions, cover and cook for 5 mins. Remove the lid and cook for 5 mins more, stirring frequently until softened. Add the garlic, chilli flakes and paprika, stir briefly, then tip in the tomatoes and a can of water. Stir in the bouillon and aubergine, then bring to a simmer, cover and cook for 20 mins.

STEP 2

Cook the penne in a pan of boiling water for 12 mins until al dente. Drain, reserving 60ml of the cooking water. Add the cooked penne to the sauce, and toss well with the basil and a little of the reserved water, if needed. Spoon into two shallow bowls, and serve topped with the cheese and some extra basil, if you like.

Mango sorbet

Prep:15 mins plus freezing

Serves 8

Ingredients

- 3 large, ripe mangoes
- 200g caster sugar
- 1 lime , juiced

Method

STEP 1

Peel the mangoes with a vegetable peeler, cut as much of the flesh away from the stone as you can, put it in a food processor or blender.

STEP 2

Add the sugar, lime juice and 200ml water. Blend for a few minutes, until the mango is very smooth and the sugar has dissolved – rub a little of the mixture between your fingers, if it still feels gritty, blend for a little longer. Pour into a container and put in the freezer for a few hours.

STEP 3

Scrape the sorbet back into the blender (if it's very solid, leave at room temperature for 5-10 mins first). Whizz until you have a slushy mixture, then pour back into the tin and freeze for another hour or so.

STEP 4

Repeat **step 3**. Freeze until solid (another hour or two). *Will keep covered in the freezer for three months.*

Vegan shepherd's pie

Prep:30 mins **Cook:**1 hr and 20 mins

Serves 8 (makes eight individual or two large pies)

Ingredients

- 1.2kg floury potatoes, such as Maris Piper or King Edward
- 50ml vegetable oil
- 30g dried porcini mushrooms, soaked in hot water for 15 mins, then drained (reserve the liquid)
- 2 large leeks, chopped
- 2 small onions, chopped
- 4 medium carrots (about 300g), cut into small cubes
- 1 vegetable stock cube (make sure it's vegan - we used Kallo)
- 3 garlic cloves, crushed
- 2 tbsp tomato purée
- 2 tsp smoked paprika
- 1 small butternut squash, peeled and cut into small cubes
- ½ small pack marjoram or oregano, leaves picked and roughly chopped
- ½ small pack thyme, leaves picked
- ½ small pack sage, leaves picked and roughly chopped
- 4 celery sticks, chopped
- 400g can chickpeas
- 300g frozen peas
- 300g frozen spinach
- 20ml olive oil
- small pack flat-leaf parsley, chopped
- tomato ketchup, to serve (optional)

Method

STEP 1

Put the unpeeled potatoes in a large saucepan, cover with water, bring to the boil and simmer for 40 mins until the skins start to split. Drain and leave to cool a little.

STEP 2

Meanwhile, heat the vegetable oil in a large heavy-based sauté pan or flameproof casserole dish. Add the mushrooms, leeks , onions, carrots and the stock cube and cook gently for 5 mins , stirring every so often. If it starts to stick, reduce the heat and stir more frequently, scraping the bits from the bottom. The veg should be soft but not mushy.

STEP 3

Add the garlic, tomato purée, paprika, squash and herbs. Stir and turn the heat up a bit, cook for 3 mins, add the celery, then stir and cook for a few more mins.

STEP 4

Tip in the chickpeas along with the water in the can and reserved mushroom stock. Add the peas and spinach and stir well. Cook for 5 mins, stirring occasionally, then season, turn off and set aside. There should still be plenty of liquid and the veg should be bright and a little firm.

STEP 5

Peel the potatoes and discard the skin. Mash 200g with a fork and stir into the veg. Break the rest of the potatoes into chunks, mix with the olive oil and parsley and season.

STEP 6

Divide the filling into the pie dishes and top with the potatotes. Heat oven to 190C/170C fan/gas 5 and bake the pies for 40-45 mins, until the top is golden and the filling is heated through. If making individual pies, check after 20 mins. Best served with tomato ketchup – as all great shepherd's pies are.

Red pepper, squash & harissa soup

Prep:15 mins **Cook:**1 hr

Serves 6

Ingredients

- 1 small butternut squash (about 600-700g), peeled and cut into chunks
- 2 red pepper , roughly chopped
- 2 red onion , roughly chopped
- 3 tbsp rapeseed oil
- 3 garlic cloves in their skins
- 1 tbsp ground coriander
- 2 tsp ground cumin
- 1.2l chicken or vegetable stock
- 2 tbsp harissa paste

- 50ml double cream

Method

STEP 1

Heat oven to 180C/160C fan/gas 4. Put all the veg on a large baking tray and toss together with rapeseed oil, garlic cloves in their skins, ground coriander, ground cumin and some seasoning. Roast for 45 mins, moving the veg around in the tray after 30 mins, until soft and starting to caramelise. Squeeze the garlic cloves out of their skins. Tip everything into a large pan. Add the chicken or vegetable stock, harissa paste and double cream. Bring to a simmer and bubble for a few mins. Blitz the soup in a blender, check the seasoning and add more liquid if you need to. Serve swirled with extra cream and harissa.

Cabbage soup

Prep:20 mins **Cook:**50 mins

Serves 6

Ingredients

- 2 tbsp olive oil
- 1 large onion , finely chopped
- 2 celery sticks , finely chopped
- 1 large carrot , finely chopped
- 70g smoked pancetta , diced (optional)
- 1 large Savoy cabbage , shredded
- 2 fat garlic cloves , crushed
- 1 heaped tsp sweet smoked paprika
- 1 tbsp finely chopped rosemary
- 1 x 400g can chopped tomatoes
- 1.7l hot vegetable stock
- 1 x 400g can chickpeas , drained and rinsed
- shaved parmesan (or vegetarian alternative), to serve (optional)
- crusty bread , to serve (optional)

Method

STEP 1

Heat the oil in a casserole pot over a low heat. Add the onion, celery and carrot, along with a generous pinch of salt, and fry gently for 15 mins, or until the veg begins to soften. If you're using pancetta, add it to the pan, turn up the heat and fry for a few mins more until turning golden brown. Tip in the cabbage and fry for 5 mins, then stir through the garlic, paprika and rosemary and cook for 1 min more.

STEP 2

Tip the chopped tomatoes and stock into the pan. Bring to a simmer, then cook, uncovered, for 30 mins, adding the chickpeas for the final 10 mins. Season generously with salt and black pepper.

STEP 3

Ladle the soup into six deep bowls. Serve with the shaved parmesan and crusty bread, if you like.

Roasted roots & sage soup

Prep:15 mins **Cook:**45 mins

Serves 2

Ingredients

- 1 parsnip , peeled and chopped
- 2 carrots , peeled and chopped
- 300g turnip , swede or celeriac, chopped
- 4 garlic cloves , skin left on
- 1 tbsp rapeseed oil , plus ½ tsp
- 1 tsp maple syrup
- ¼ small bunch of sage , leaves picked, 4 whole, the rest finely chopped
- 750ml vegetable stock
- grating of nutmeg
- 1½ tbsp fat-free yogurt

Method

STEP 1

Heat the oven to 200C/180C fan/gas 6. Toss the root vegetables and garlic with 1 tbsp oil and season. Tip onto a baking tray and roast for 30 mins until tender. Toss with the maple syrup and the chopped sage, then roast for another 10 mins until golden and glazed. Brush the whole sage leaves with ½ tsp oil and add to the baking tray in the last 3-4 mins to crisp up, then remove and set aside.

STEP 2

Scrape the vegetables into a pan, squeeze the garlic out of the skins, discarding the papery shells, and add with the stock, then blend with a stick blender until very smooth and creamy. Bring to a simmer and season with salt, pepper and nutmeg.

STEP 3

Divide between bowls. Serve with a swirl of yogurt and the crispy sage leaves.

Artichoke & aubergine rice

Prep:15 mins **Cook:**50 mins

Serves 6

Ingredients

- 60ml olive oil
- 2 aubergines , cut into chunks
- 1 large onion , finely chopped
- 2 garlic cloves , crushed
- small pack parsley , leaves picked, stalks finely chopped
- 2 tsp smoked paprika
- 2 tsp turmeric
- 400g paella rice
- 1 ½l Kallo vegetable stock
- 2 x 175g packs chargrilled artichokes
- 2 lemons 1 juiced, 1 cut into wedges to serve

Method

STEP 1

Heat 2 tbsp of the oil in a large non-stick frying pan or paella pan. Fry the aubergines until nicely coloured on all sides (add another tbsp of oil if the aubergine begins catching too much), then remove and set aside. Add another tbsp of oil to the pan and lightly fry the onion for 2-3 mins or until softened. Add the garlic and parsley stalks, cook for a few mins more, then stir in the spices and rice until everything is well coated. Heat for 2 mins, add half the stock and cook, uncovered, over a medium heat for 20 mins, stirring occasionally to prevent it from sticking.

STEP 2

Nestle the aubergine and artichokes into the mixture, pour over the rest of the stock and cook for 20 mins more or until the rice is cooked through. Chop the parsley leaves, stir through with the lemon juice and season well. Bring the whole pan to the table and spoon into bowls, with the lemon wedges on the side.

Hearty lentil one pot

Prep:10 mins **Cook:**1 hr

Serves 4

Ingredients

- 40g dried porcini mushrooms , roughly chopped
- 200g dried brown lentils
- 1 ½ tbsp chopped rosemary
- 3 tbsp rapeseed oil
- 2 large onions , roughly chopped
- 150g chestnut baby button mushrooms
- 4 garlic cloves , finely grated
- 2 tbsp vegetable bouillon powder
- 2 large carrots (350g), cut into chunks
- 3 celery sticks (165g), chopped
- 500g potatoes , cut into chunks
- 200g cavolo nero , shredded

Method

STEP 1

Cover the mushrooms in boiling water and leave to soak for 10 mins. Boil the lentils in a pan with plenty of water for 10 mins. Drain and rinse, then tip into a pan with the dried mushrooms and soaking water (don't add the last bit of the liquid as it can contain some grit), rosemary and 2 litres water. Season, cover and simmer for 20 mins.

STEP 2

Meanwhile, heat the oil in a large pan and fry the onions for 5 mins. Stir in the fresh mushrooms and garlic and fry for 5 mins more. Stir in the lentil mixture and bouillon powder, then add the carrots, celery and potatoes. Cover and cook for 20 mins, stirring often, until the veg and lentils are tender, topping up the water level if needed.

STEP 3

Remove any tough stalks from the cavolo nero, then add to the pan and cover and cook for 5 mins more. If you're following our Healthy Diet Plan, serve half in bowls, then chill the rest to eat another day. *Will keep in the fridge for two to three days.* Reheat in a pan until hot.

Spiced carrot & lentil soup

Prep:10 mins **Cook:**15 mins

Serves 4

Ingredients

- 2 tsp cumin seeds
- pinch chilli flakes

- 2 tbsp olive oil
- 600g carrots, washed and coarsely grated (no need to peel)
- 140g split red lentils
- 1l hot vegetable stock (from a cube is fine)
- 125ml milk (to make it dairy-free, see 'try' below)
- plain yogurt and naan bread, to serve

Method

STEP 1

Heat a large saucepan and dry-fry 2 tsp cumin seeds and a pinch of chilli flakes for 1 min, or until they start to jump around the pan and release their aromas.

STEP 2

Scoop out about half with a spoon and set aside. Add 2 tbsp olive oil, 600g coarsely grated carrots, 140g split red lentils, 1l hot vegetable stock and 125ml milk to the pan and bring to the boil.

STEP 3

Simmer for 15 mins until the lentils have swollen and softened.

STEP 4

Whizz the soup with a stick blender or in a food processor until smooth (or leave it chunky if you prefer).

STEP 5

Season to taste and finish with a dollop of plain yogurt and a sprinkling of the reserved toasted spices. Serve with warmed naan breads.

Chana masala with pomegranate raita

Prep:10 mins **Cook:**35 mins

Serves 2

Ingredients

- 1 tbsp rapeseed oil
- 2 onions , halved and thinly sliced
- 1 tbsp chopped ginger
- 2 large garlic cloves , finely grated or crushed
- 1 green chilli , halved, deseeded and thinly sliced
- ½ tsp cumin seeds

- ½ tsp mustard seeds
- ½ tsp garam masala
- ½ tsp turmeric
- 1 tsp ground coriander
- 400g can chickpeas , undrained
- 4 small tomatoes (about 160g), cut into wedges
- 2 tsp vegetable bouillon powder
- cooked wholegrain rice , to serve (optional)

For the pomegranate raita

- 150ml plain bio yogurt
- 25g pomegranate seeds
- 2 tbsp finely chopped coriander , plus extra leaves to serve

Method

STEP 1

Heat the oil in a large non-stick pan, then cook the onions, ginger, garlic and chilli for 15-20 mins.

STEP 2

Add the spices, chickpeas, the liquid from the can, ¾ can cold water, the tomatoes and bouillon. Cover and simmer for 10 mins.

STEP 3

Meanwhile, mix the ingredients for the raita in a small bowl, reserving a few coriander leaves. Roughly mash some of the curry to thicken it. Spoon into bowls with rice, if you like. Scatter over the reserved coriander and serve with the raita on the side.

Prosciutto, kale & butter bean stew

Prep:5 mins **Cook:**20 mins

Serves 4

Ingredients

- 80g pack prosciutto , torn into pieces
- 2 tbsp olive oil
- 1 fennel bulb , sliced
- 2 garlic clove , crushed
- 1 tsp chilli flakes

- 4 thyme sprigs
- 150ml white wine or chicken stock
- 2 x 400g cans butter beans
- 400g can cherry tomatoes
- 200g bag sliced kale

Method

STEP 1

Fry the prosciutto in a dry saucepan over a high heat until crisp, then remove half with a slotted spoon and set aside. Turn the heat down to low, pour in the oil and tip in the fennel with a pinch of salt. Cook for 5 mins until softened, then throw in the garlic, chilli flakes and thyme and cook for a further 2 mins, then pour in the wine or stock and bring to a simmer.

STEP 2

Tip both cans of butter beans into the stew, along with their liquid, then add the tomatoes, season well and bring everything to a simmer. Cook, undisturbed, for 5 mins, then stir through the kale. Once wilted, ladle the stew into bowls, removing the thyme sprigs and topping each portion with the remaining prosciutto.

Leek, pea & watercress soup

Prep:10 mins **Cook:**22 mins

Serves 4

Ingredients

- 1 tbsp olive oil , plus a drizzle to serve
- 2 leeks , finely sliced
- 4 small garlic cloves , crushed
- 650-800ml hot veg stock
- 80g watercress
- 400g frozen peas
- 1 small lemon , zested and juiced
- small bunch of parsley , finely chopped
- dairy-free crème fraîche and crusty bread, to serve (optional)

Method

STEP 1

Heat the oil in a large saucepan over a medium heat. Add the leeks and garlic and fry for 7-10 mins or until softened and translucent.

STEP 2

Pour in the hot stock and simmer for 5-10 mins. Stir through the watercress, reserving a few leaves for garnish, then the peas, and cook for 5 mins until wilted. Use a hand blender or processor and whizz until smooth. Stir through the lemon juice and zest, then season to taste. Stir through half the parsley. Ladle into bowls and top with the remaining parsley, reserved watercress and a drizzle of olive oil. Swirl through some crème fraîche, then serve with crusty bread, if you like.

Easy slow cooker chicken casserole

Prep:10 mins **Cook:**4 hrs - 8 hrs

Serves 4

Ingredients

- 1 leek, roughly chopped
- 1 carrot, roughly chopped
- 1 onion, roughly chopped
- 350g new potatoes, roughly chopped
- 6 skinless, boneless chicken thighs, chopped
- 500ml chicken stock
- 4 tbsp vegetable gravy granules

Method

STEP 1

Put the veg and chicken in a slow cooker. Pour the stock over and around the chicken thighs, then mix in the gravy granules to thicken it up (the sauce will be quite thick – use less gravy if you prefer a runnier casserole).

STEP 2

Switch the slow cooker to low and leave to cook for at least 4 hrs, or up to 8 hrs – try putting it on before you go to work, so that it's ready when you get home. Season well, then serve.

Spiced chicken, spinach & sweet potato stew

Prep:15 mins **Cook:**40 mins

Serves 4

Ingredients

- 3 sweet potatoes, cut into chunks
- 190g bag spinach
- 1 tbsp sunflower oil
- 8 chicken thighs, skinless and boneless
- 500ml chicken stock
- For the spice paste
- 2 onions, chopped
- 1 red chilli, chopped
- 1 tsp paprika
- thumb-sized piece ginger, grated
- 400g can tomatoes
- 2 preserved lemons, deseeded and chopped

To serve

- pumpkin seeds, toasted
- 2-3 preserved lemons, deseeded and chopped
- 4 naan bread, warmed

Method

STEP 1

Put the sweet potato in a large, deep saucepan over a high heat. Cover with boiling water and boil for 10 mins. Meanwhile, put all the paste ingredients in a food processor and blend until very finely chopped. Set aside until needed.

STEP 2

Put the spinach in a large colander in the sink and pour the sweet potatoes and their cooking water over it to drain the potatoes and wilt the spinach at the same time. Leave to steam-dry.

STEP 3

Return the saucepan to the heat (no need to wash it first), then add the oil, followed by the spice paste. Fry the paste for about 5 mins until thickened, then add the chicken. Fry for 8-10 mins until the chicken starts to colour. Pour over the stock, bring to the boil and leave to simmer for 10 mins, stirring occasionally.

STEP 4

Check the chicken is cooked by cutting into one of the thighs and making sure it's white throughout with no signs of pink. Season with black pepper, then add the sweet potato. Leave to simmer for a further 5 mins. Meanwhile, roughly chop the spinach and add to the stew. *At this point you can leave the stew to cool and freeze for up to 3 months, if you like.*

STEP 5

Scatter over the pumpkin seeds and preserved lemons, and serve with warm naan bread on the side.

Creamy chicken & asparagus braise

Prep:10 mins **Cook:**20 mins - 25 mins

Serves 2

Ingredients

- 1 tbsp rapeseed oil
- 2 skinless chicken breasts (about 150g each)
- 10 medium asparagus spears , each cut into 3
- 1 large or 2 small leeks , well washed and thickly sliced
- 3 celery sticks , sliced
- 200ml reduced-salt vegetable bouillon
- 140g frozen peas
- 1 egg yolk
- 4 tbsp natural bio yogurt
- 1 garlic clove , finely grated
- ⅓ small pack fresh tarragon , chopped
- new potatoes , to serve (optional)

Method

STEP 1

Heat the oil in a large non-stick frying pan and fry the chicken for 5 mins, turning to brown both sides.

STEP 2

Add the asparagus (reserve the tips), leeks and celery, pour in the bouillon and simmer for 10 mins. Add the asparagus tips and peas, and cook for 5 mins more.

STEP 3

Meanwhile, stir the egg yolk with the yogurt and garlic. Stir the yogurt mixture into the vegetables and add the tarragon. Divide between two warm plates, then place the chicken on top of the vegetables. Serve with new potatoes, if you like.

Prawn jambalaya

Prep:10 mins **Cook:**35 mins

Serves 2

Ingredients

- 1 tbsp rapeseed oil
- 1 onion , chopped
- 3 celery sticks , sliced
- 100g wholegrain basmati rice
- 1 tsp mild chilli powder
- 1 tbsp ground coriander
- ½ tsp fennel seeds
- 400g can chopped tomatoes
- 1 tsp vegetable bouillon powder
- 1 yellow pepper , roughly chopped
- 2 garlic cloves , chopped
- 1 tbsp fresh thyme leaves
- 150g pack small prawns , thawed if frozen
- 3 tbsp chopped parsley

Method

STEP 1

Heat the oil in a large, deep frying pan. Add the onion and celery, and fry for 5 mins to soften. Add the rice and spices, and pour in the tomatoes with just under 1 can of water. Stir in the bouillon powder, pepper, garlic and thyme.

STEP 2

Cover the pan with a lid and simmer for 30 mins until the rice is tender and almost all the liquid has been absorbed. Stir in the prawns and parsley, cook briefly to heat through, then serve.

Asparagus & broad bean lasagne

Prep:35 mins **Cook:**1 hr and 10 mins

Serves 4

Ingredients

- 225ml whole milk
- 320g frozen baby broad beans
- 3 garlic cloves , chopped
- 30g pack fresh basil , roughly chopped
- ½ lemon , zested
- 4 spring onions , chopped

- 1 tsp vegetable bouillon powder
- 6 wholemeal lasagne sheets
- 320g frozen peas
- 2 x 300g tubs low-fat cottage cheese
- 1 egg
- whole nutmeg , for grating
- 250g asparagus , woody ends trimmed
- 25g parmesan or vegetarian alternative, finely grated

Method

STEP 1

Heat oven to 180C/160C fan/gas 4. Heat the milk in a pan until just boiling, then tip in the beans (add a splash of water to cover if you need to). Cook for 3 mins to defrost, then add the garlic, basil, lemon zest, spring onions and bouillon, then blitz for a few mins with a hand blender until smooth.

STEP 2

Spoon half the purée into a 20 x 26cm ovenproof dish. Top with 3 lasagne sheets, the remaining purée, and the peas, then the remaining lasagne sheets.

STEP 3

Whisk the cottage cheese with the egg and a good grating of nutmeg. Pour over the lasagne, then press in the asparagus and scatter over the parmesan. Bake for 1 hr until golden and a knife easily slides through. *Can be kept chilled for two days.*

Mediterranean turkey-stuffed peppers

Prep:20 mins **Cook:**30 mins

Serves 2

Ingredients

- 2 red peppers (about 220g)
- 1 ½ tbsp olive oil, plus an extra drizzle
- 240g lean turkey breast mince (under 8% fat)
- ½ small onion, chopped
- 1 garlic clove, grated
- 1 tsp ground cumin
- 3-4 mushrooms, sliced
- 400g can chopped tomatoes

- 1 tbsp tomato purée
- 1 chicken stock cube
- handful fresh oregano leaves
- 60g mozzarella, grated
- 150g green vegetables (spinach, kale, broccoli, mangetout or green beans), to serve

Method

STEP 1

Heat oven to 190C/170C fan/gas 5. Halve the peppers lengthways, then remove the seeds and core but keep the stalks on. Rub the peppers with a drizzle of olive oil and season well. Put on a baking tray and roast for 15 mins.

STEP 2

Meanwhile, heat 1 tbsp olive oil in a large pan over a medium heat. Fry the mince for 2-3 mins, stirring to break up the chunks, then tip onto a plate.

STEP 3

Wipe out your pan, then heat the rest of the oil over a medium-high heat. Add the onion and garlic, stir-fry for 2-3 mins, then add the cumin and mushrooms and cook for 2-3 mins more.

STEP 4

Tip the mince back into the pan and add the chopped tomatoes and tomato purée. Crumble in the stock cube and cook for 3-4 mins, then add the oregano and season. Remove the peppers from the oven and fill them with as much of the mince as you can. (Don't worry if some spills out it – it will go satisfyingly crisp in the oven.) Top with the cheese and return to the oven for 10-15 mins until the cheese starts to turn golden.

STEP 5

Carefully slide the peppers onto a plate and serve alongside a pile of your favourite greens blanched, boiled or steamed.

Super-quick sesame ramen

Prep:5 mins **Cook:**10 mins

Serves 1

Ingredients

- 80g pack instant noodles (look for an Asian brand with a flavour like sesame)
- 2 spring onions , finely chopped

- ½ head pak choi
- 1 egg
- 1 tsp sesame seeds
- chilli sauce , to serve

Method

STEP 1

Cook the noodles with the sachet of flavouring provided (or use stock instead of the sachet, if you have it). Add the spring onions and pak choi for the final min.

STEP 2

Meanwhile, simmer the egg for 6 mins from boiling, run it under cold water to stop it cooking, then peel it. Toast the sesame seeds in a frying pan.

STEP 3

Tip the noodles and greens into a deep bowl, halve the boiled egg and place on top. Sprinkle with sesame seeds, then drizzle with the sauce or sesame oil provided with the noodles, and chilli sauce, if using.

Ginger, sesame and chilli prawn & broccoli stir-fry

Prep:5 mins **Cook:**10 mins

Serves 2

Ingredients

- 250g broccoli , thin-stemmed if you like, cut into even-sized florets
- 2 balls stem ginger , finely chopped, plus 2 tbsp syrup from the jar
- 3 tbsp low-salt soy sauce
- 1 garlic clove , crushed
- 1 red chilli , a little thinly sliced, the rest deseeded and finely chopped
- 2 tsp sesame seeds
- ½ tbsp sesame oil
- 200g raw king prawns
- 100g beansprouts
- cooked rice or noodles, to serve

Method

STEP 1

Heat a pan of water until boiling. Tip in the broccoli and cook for just 1 min – it should still have a good crunch. Meanwhile, mix the stem ginger and syrup, soy sauce, garlic and finely chopped chilli.

STEP 2

Toast the sesame seeds in a dry wok or large frying pan. When they're nicely browned, turn up the heat and add the oil, prawns and cooked broccoli. Stir-fry for a few mins until the prawns turn pink. Pour over the ginger sauce, then tip in the beansprouts. Cook for 30 seconds, or until the beansprouts are heated thoroughly, adding a splash more soy or ginger syrup, if you like. Scatter with the sliced chilli and serve over rice or noodles.

Slow cooker shepherd's pie

Prep:1 hr **Cook:**5 hrs

Serves 4

Ingredients

- 1 tbsp olive oil
- 1 onion, finely chopped
- 3-4 thyme sprigs
- 2 carrots, finely diced
- 250g lean (10%) mince lamb or beef
- 1 tbsp plain flour
- 1 tbsp tomato purée
- 400g can lentils, or white beans
- 1 tsp Worcestershire sauce

For the topping

- 650g potatoes, peeled and cut into chunks
- 250g sweet potatoes, peeled and cut into chunks
- 2 tbsp half-fat crème fraîche

Method

STEP 1

Heat the slow cooker if necessary. Heat the oil in a large frying pan. Tip the onions and thyme sprigs and fry for 2-3 mins. Then add the carrots and fry together, stirring occasionally until the vegetables start to brown. Stir in the mince and fry for 1-2 mins until no longer pink. Stir in the flour then cook for another 1-2 mins. Stir in the tomato purée and lentils and season with pepper and the Worcestershire sauce, adding a splash of water if you think the mixture is too dry. Scrape everything into the slow cooker.

STEP 2

Meanwhile cook both lots of potatoes in simmering water for 12-13 minutes or until they are cooked through. Drain well and then mash with the crème fraîche. Spoon this on top of the mince mixture and cook on Low for 5 hours - the mixture should be bubbling at the sides when it is ready. Crisp up the potato topping under the grill if you like.

Vietnamese chicken noodle soup

Prep:20 mins **Cook:**25 mins

Serves 6

Ingredients

- 1 tbsp vegetable oil
- 3 shallots, sliced
- 3 garlic cloves, sliced
- 1 lemongrass stalk, chopped
- 2.5cm piece ginger, sliced
- 3 star anise
- 1 cinnamon stick
- 1 tsp coriander seeds
- ¼ tsp Chinese five spice
- ¼ tsp black peppercorns
- 1 tsp caster sugar
- 1 tbsp fish sauce
- 1.25 - 1.5 litres good quality fresh chicken stock
- 3 large chicken breasts (about 500g)

To serve

- 450g rice noodles
- 4 spring onions, finely sliced on an angle
- 1 carrot, shredded or peeled into ribbon with a vegetable peeler
- 2 large handfuls (150g) mung bean sprouts
- large bunch coriander, chopped
- small bunch mint, leaves chopped
- 1 red chilli, thinly sliced (optional)
- 2 tbsp crispy fried shallots (optional)
- 1 kaffir lime leaf, tough central stalk removed, very finely sliced, (optional)
- 1 lime, cut into wedges

Method

STEP 1

Heat the oil in a small frying pan on medium heat and gently cook the shallots and garlic until caramelised and golden brown (about 4-5 mins).

STEP 2

In a large saucepan, add the caramelised shallots and garlic, lemongrass, ginger, star anise, cinnamon stick, coriander seeds, Chinese five-spice, peppercorns, sugar, fish sauce, chicken stock and chicken breasts. Cover with a lid and bring to a very gentle simmer for about 15 mins.

STEP 3

Meanwhile, cook the noodles, following pack instructions, until just cooked through (do not over-cook). Rinse under cold water to prevent them sticking together. Drain and divide between serving bowls.

STEP 4

Strain the soup through a sieve. Discard the spices. Shred the chicken and keep to one side. Return soup to the pot and bring to a boil. Season to taste with more fish sauce if needed.

STEP 5

To serve, ladle piping hot soup into bowls of noodles and chicken, and top with spring onion, carrot, bean sprouts, and herbs, plus the chilli, crispy shallots and kaffir lime leaf if using. Serve with a lime wedge to squeeze over, and more fish sauce and chilli to taste.

Cod with cucumber, avocado & mango salsa salad

Prep:5 mins **Cook:**8 mins

Serves 2

Ingredients

- 2 x skinless cod fillets
- 1 lime , zested and juiced
- 1 small mango , peeled, stoned and chopped (or 2 peaches, stoned and chopped)
- 1 small avocado , stoned, peeled and sliced
- ¼ cucumber , chopped
- 160g cherry tomatoes , quartered
- 1 red chilli , deseeded and chopped
- 2 spring onions , sliced
- handful chopped coriander

Method

STEP 1

Heat oven to 200C/180C fan/gas 6. Put the fish in a shallow ovenproof dish and pour over half the lime juice, with a little of the zest, then grind over some black pepper. Bake for 8 mins or until the fish flakes easily but is still moist.

STEP 2

Meanwhile, put the rest of the ingredients, plus the remaining lime juice and zest, in a bowl and combine well. Spoon onto plates and top with the cod, spooning over any juices in the dish.

Easy soup maker lentil soup

Prep:5 mins **Cook:**30 mins

Serves 4

Ingredients

- 750ml vegetable or ham stock
- 75g red lentils
- 3 carrots , finely chopped
- 1 medium leek , sliced (150g)
- small handful chopped parsley , to serve

Method

STEP 1

Put the stock, lentils, carrots and leek into a soup maker, and press the 'chunky soup' function. Make sure you don't fill it above the max fill line. The soup will look a little foamy to start, but don't worry – it will disappear once cooked.

STEP 2

Once the cycle is complete, check the lentils are tender, and season well. Scatter over the parsley to serve.

Singapore noodles with prawns

Prep:10 mins **Cook:**10 mins

Serves 2

Ingredients

- 2 nests thin vermicelli rice noodles
- 1 tbsp light soy sauce
- 1 tbsp oyster sauce
- 2 tsp mild curry powder
- 1 tbsp sesame oil
- 1 garlic clove , chopped
- 1 red chilli , thinly sliced (deseeded if you don't like it too hot)
- thumb-sized piece ginger , grated
- 1 medium onion , sliced
- 1 red pepper or yellow pepper, cut into thin batons
- 4 spring onions , cut in half lengthways then into batons
- 8 raw king prawns
- 1 large egg , beaten
- coriander leaves, to serve

Method

STEP 1

Soak the rice noodles in warm water for 5 mins until softened but still al dente. Drain and set aside.

STEP 2

In a small bowl, mix together the soy, oyster sauce and curry powder.

STEP 3

In a large wok, add half the oil and fry the garlic, chilli and ginger until golden, about 2 mins. Add the remaining oil, onion, pepper, spring onions, prawns and noodles and stir-fry for a few mins. Push everything to one side, add the egg and scramble. Add the soy sauce mixture, toss again for a few more mins, then remove from the heat. Sprinkle over the coriander leaves before serving.

Ginger chicken & green bean noodles

Prep:10 mins **Cook:**15 mins

Serves 2

Ingredients

- ½ tbsp vegetable oil
- 2 skinless chicken breasts, sliced
- 200g green beans , trimmed and halved crosswise
- thumb-sized piece of ginger , peeled and cut into matchsticks

- 2 garlic cloves , sliced
- 1 ball stem ginger , finely sliced, plus 1 tsp syrup from the jar
- 1 tsp cornflour , mixed with 1 tbsp water
- 1 tsp dark soy sauce , plus extra to serve (optional)
- 2 tsp rice vinegar
- 200g cooked egg noodles

Method

STEP 1

Heat the oil in a wok over a high heat and stir-fry the chicken for 5 mins. Add the green beans and stir-fry for 4-5 mins more until the green beans are just tender, and the chicken is just cooked through.

STEP 2

Stir in the fresh ginger and garlic, and stir-fry for 2 mins, then add the stem ginger and syrup, the cornflour mix, soy sauce and vinegar. Stir-fry for 1 min, then toss in the noodles. Cook until everything is hot and the sauce coats the noodles. Drizzle with more soy, if you like, and serve.

Spicy meatballs with chilli black beans

Prep:20 mins **Cook:**25 mins

Serves 4

Ingredients

- 1 red onion, halved and sliced
- 2 garlic cloves, sliced
- 1 large yellow pepper, quartered, deseeded and diced
- 1 tsp ground cumin
- 2-3 tsp chipotle chilli paste
- 300ml reduced-salt chicken stock
- 400g can cherry tomatoes
- 400g can black beans or red kidney beans, drained
- 1 avocado, stoned, peeled and chopped
- juice ½ lime

For the meatballs

- 500g pack turkey breast mince
- 50g porridge oats
- 2 spring onions, finely chopped

- 1 tsp ground cumin
- 1 tsp coriander
- small bunch coriander, chopped, stalks and leaves kept separate
- 1 tsp rapeseed oil

Method

STEP 1

First make the meatballs. Tip the mince into a bowl, add the oats, spring onions, spices and the coriander stalks, then lightly knead the ingredients together until well mixed. Shape into 12 ping-pong- sized balls. Heat the oil in a non-stick frying pan, add the meatballs and cook, turning them frequently, until golden. Remove from the pan.

STEP 2

Tip the onion and garlic into the pan with the pepper and stir-fry until softened. Stir in the cumin and chilli paste, then pour in the stock. Return the meatballs to the pan and cook, covered, over a low heat for 10 mins. Stir in the tomatoes and beans, and cook, uncovered, for a few mins more. Toss the avocado chunks in the lime juice and serve the meatballs topped with the avocado and coriander leaves.

Yaki udon

Prep:10 mins **Cook:**5 mins

Serves 2

Ingredients

- 250g dried udon noodles (400g frozen or fresh)
- 2 tbsp sesame oil
- 1 onion, thickly sliced
- ¼ head white cabbage, roughly sliced
- 10 shiitake mushrooms
- 4 spring onions, finely sliced
- For the sauce
- 4 tbsp mirin
- 2 tbsp soy sauce
- 1 tbsp caster sugar
- 1 tbsp Worcestershire sauce (or vegetarian alternative)

Method

STEP 1

Boil some water in a large saucepan. Add 250ml cold water and the udon noodles. (As they are so thick, adding cold water helps them to cook a little bit slower so the middle cooks through). If using frozen or fresh noodles, cook for 2 mins or until al dente; dried will take longer, about 5-6 mins. Drain and leave in the colander.

STEP 2

Heat 1 tbsp of the oil, add the onion and cabbage and sauté for 5 mins until softened. Add the mushrooms and some spring onions, and sauté for 1 more min. Pour in the remaining sesame oil and the noodles. If using cold noodles, let them heat through before adding the ingredients for the sauce – otherwise tip in straight away and keep stir-frying until sticky and piping hot. Sprinkle with the remaining spring onions.

Basic lentils

Prep:10 mins **Cook:**45 mins

Makes 6 portions

Ingredients

- 2 tbsp coconut oil
- 2 onions , chopped
- 4 garlic cloves , chopped
- large piece of ginger , chopped
- 300g red split lentils
- 1 tsp turmeric
- 2 tomatoes , roughly chopped
- 1 tsp coriander seeds
- 1 tsp cumin seeds
- 1 tsp black mustard seeds
- 1 lemon , juiced

Method

STEP 1

Melt 1 tbsp coconut oil in a large saucepan. Add the onion and a pinch of salt, and cook for 8 mins. Stir in the garlic and ginger and cook for a few mins more. Add the lentils, turmeric and tomatoes, stir to combine, then pour in 1 litre of water. Bring to the boil, then turn down and simmer for 25-30 mins, stirring occasionally, until the lentils are tender.

STEP 2

Heat the rest of the oil in a frying pan. When it's very hot, add the spices and fry for a min or so until fragrant, then stir them through. Add the lemon juice and season to taste. Will keep for four days in the fridge, or freeze it in batches and use to make our lentil kedgeree, lentil fritters, or spinach dhal with harissa yogurt.

Baked piri-piri tilapia with crushed potatoes

Prep:10 mins **Cook:**25 mins

Serves 4

Ingredients

- 600g small new potatoes
- 2 red peppers, cut into chunky pieces
- 1 tbsp red wine vinegar
- drizzle of extra virgin olive oil
- 4 large pieces tilapia or cod
- green salad, to serve

For the piri-piri sauce

- 6 hot pickled peppers (I used Peppadew)
- 1 tsp chilli flakes
- 2 garlic cloves
- juice and zest 1 lemon
- 1 tbsp red wine vinegar
- 2 tbsp extra virgin olive oil
- 1 tbsp smoked paprika

Method

STEP 1

Heat oven to 220C/200C fan/gas 7. Boil the potatoes until knife-tender, then drain. Spread out on a large baking tray and gently crush with the back of a spatula. Add the peppers, drizzle with the vinegar and oil, season well and roast for 25 mins.

STEP 2

Put the piri-piri ingredients in a food processor with some salt. Purée until fine, then pour into a bowl. Put the fish on a baking tray and spoon over some of the piri-piri sauce. Season and bake for the final 10 mins of the potatoes' cooking time. Serve everything with the extra sauce and a green salad on the side.

Parma pork with potato salad

Prep:15 mins **Cook:**15 mins

Serves 2

Ingredients

- 175g new potatoes (we used Jersey Royals), scrubbed and thickly sliced
- 3 celery sticks, thickly sliced
- 3 tbsp bio yogurt
- 2 gherkins (about 85g each), sliced
- ¼ tsp caraway seeds
- ½ tsp Dijon mustard
- 2 x 100g pieces lean pork tenderloin
- 2 tsp chopped sage
- 2 slices Parma ham
- 1 tsp rapeseed oil
- 2 tsp balsamic vinegar
- 2 handfuls salad leaves

Method

STEP 1

Bring a pan of water to the boil, add the potatoes and celery and cook for 8 mins. Meanwhile, mix the yogurt, guerkins, caraway and mustard in a bowl. When the potatoes and celery are cooked, drain and set aside for a few mins to cool a little.

STEP 2

Bash the pork pieces with a rolling pin to flatten them. Sprinkle over the sage and some pepper, then top each with a slice of Parma ham. Heat the oil in a non-stick pan, add the pork and cook for a couple of mins each side, turning carefully. Add the balsamic vinegar and let it sizzle in the pan.

STEP 3

Stir the potatoes and celery into the dressing and serve with the pork, with some salad leaves on the side.

Red lentil, chickpea & chilli soup

Prep:10 mins **Cook:**25 mins

Serves 4

Ingredients

- 2 tsp cumin seeds

- large pinch chilli flakes
- 1 tbsp olive oil
- 1 red onion, chopped
- 140g red split lentils
- 850ml vegetable stock or water
- 400g can tomatoes, whole or chopped
- 200g can chickpeas or ½ a can, drained and rinsed (freeze leftovers)
- small bunch coriander, roughly chopped (save a few leaves, to serve)
- 4 tbsp 0% Greek yogurt, to serve

Method

STEP 1

Heat a large saucepan and dry-fry 2 tsp cumin seeds and a large pinch of chilli flakes for 1 min, or until they start to jump around the pan and release their aromas.

STEP 2

Add 1 tbsp olive oil and 1 chopped red onion, and cook for 5 mins.

STEP 3

Stir in 140g red split lentils, 850ml vegetable stock or water and a 400g can tomatoes, then bring to the boil. Simmer for 15 mins until the lentils have softened.

STEP 4

Whizz the soup with a stick blender or in a food processor until it is a rough purée, pour back into the pan and add a 200g can drained and rinsed chickpeas.

STEP 5

Heat gently, season well and stir in a small bunch of chopped coriander, reserving a few leaves to serve. Finish with 4 tbsp 0% Greek yogurt and extra coriander leaves.

Low-sugar lime & basil green juice

Prep:5 mins no cook

Serves 1

Ingredients

- 70ml chilled apple and elderflower juice
- 50g baby spinach

- 20g basil leaves
- 6cm piece of cucumber (about 100g), chopped
- 1 lime , zested and juiced

Method

STEP 1

Pour the apple juice into a large jug then add the spinach, basil, cucumber, lime and 100ml chilled water.

STEP 2

Blitz really well with a hand blender until very smooth. Pour into a glass and drink straightaway.

Rustic vegetable soup

Prep: 15 mins **Cook:** 30 mins

Serves 4

Ingredients

- 1 tbsp rapeseed oil
- 1 large onion, chopped
- 2 carrots, chopped
- 2 celery sticks, chopped
- 50g dried red lentils
- 1½ l boiling vegetable bouillon (we used Marigold)
- 2 tbsp tomato purée
- 1 tbsp chopped fresh thyme
- 1 leek, finely sliced
- 175g bite-sized cauliflower florets
- 1 courgette, chopped
- 3 garlic cloves, finely chopped
- ½ large Savoy cabbage, stalks removed and leaves chopped
- 1 tbsp basil, chopped

Method

STEP 1

Heat the oil in a large pan with a lid. Add the onion, carrots and celery and fry for 10 mins, stirring from time to time until they are starting to colour a little around the edges. Stir in the lentils and cook for 1 min more.

STEP 2

Pour in the hot bouillon, add the tomato purée and thyme and stir well. Add the leek, cauliflower, courgette, and garlic, bring to the boil, then cover and leave to simmer for 15 mins.

STEP 3

Add the cabbage and basil and cook for 5 mins more until the veg is just tender. Season with pepper, ladle into bowls and serve. *Will keep in the fridge for a couple of days. Freezes well. Thaw, then reheat in a pan until piping hot.*

Garlicky mushroom penne

Prep:20 mins **Cook:**15 mins

Serves 2

Ingredients

- 210g can chickpeas , no need to drain
- 1 tbsp lemon juice
- 1 large garlic clove
- 1 tsp vegetable bouillon
- 2 tsp tahini
- ¼ tsp ground coriander
- 115g wholemeal penne
- 2 tsp rapeseed oil
- 2 red onions , halved and sliced
- 200g closed cup mushrooms , roughly chopped
- ½ lemon , juiced
- generous handful chopped parsley

Method

STEP 1

To make the hummus, tip a 210g can chickpeas with the liquid into a bowl and add 1 tbsp lemon juice, 1 large garlic clove, 1 tsp vegetable bouillon, 2 tsp tahini and ¼ tsp ground coriander.

STEP 2

Blitz to a wet paste with a hand blender, still retaining some texture from the chickpeas.

STEP 3

Cook 115g wholemeal penne pasta according to the pack instructions.

STEP 4

Meanwhile, heat 2 tsp rapeseed oil in a non-stick wok or large frying pan and add 2 halved and sliced red onions and 200g roughly chopped closed cup mushrooms, stirring frequently until softened and starting to caramelise.

STEP 5

Toss together lightly, squeeze over the juice of ½ a lemon and serve, adding a dash of water to loosen the mixture a little if needed. Scatter with a generous handful of chopped parsley.

Miso aubergines

Prep:5 mins **Cook:**50 mins

Serves 2

Ingredients

- 2 small aubergines, halved
- vegetable oil, for roasting and frying
- 50g brown miso
- 100g giant couscous
- 1 red chilli, thinly sliced
- ½ small pack coriander, leaves chopped

Method

STEP 1

Heat oven to 180C/160C fan/ gas 4. With a sharp knife, criss-cross the flesh of the aubergines in a diagonal pattern, then place on a baking tray. Brush the flesh with 1 tbsp vegetable oil.

STEP 2

Mix the miso with 25ml water to make a thick paste. Spread the paste over the aubergines, then cover the tray with foil and roast in the centre of the oven for 30 mins.

STEP 3

Remove the foil and roast the aubergines for a further 15-20 mins, depending on their size, until tender.

STEP 4

Meanwhile, bring a saucepan of salted water to the boil and heat 1 /2 tbsp vegetable oil over a medium-high heat in a frying pan. Add the couscous to the frying pan, toast for 2 mins until golden brown, then tip into the pan of boiling water and cook for 8-10 mins until tender (or following pack instructions). Drain well. Serve the aubergines with the couscous, topped with the chilli and a scattering of coriander leaves.

Balsamic beef with beetroot & rocket

Prep:15 mins **Cook:**25 mins

Serves 2

Ingredients

- 240g beef sirloin , fat trimmed
- 1 tbsp balsamic vinegar
- 2 tsp thyme leaves
- 2 garlic cloves , 1 finely grated, 1 sliced
- 2 tsp rapeseed oil
- 2 red onions , halved and sliced
- 175g fine beans , trimmed
- 2 cooked beetroot , halved and cut into wedges
- 6 pitted Kalamata olives , quartered
- 2 handfuls rocket

Method

STEP 1

Beat the steak with a rolling pin until it is about the thickness of two £1 coins, then cut into two equal pieces. In a bowl, mix the balsamic, thyme, grated garlic, half the oil and a grinding of black pepper. Place the steaks in the marinade and set aside.

STEP 2

Heat the remaining 1 tsp oil in a large non-stick frying pan, and fry the onions and garlic for 8-10 mins, stirring frequently, until soft and starting to brown. Meanwhile, steam the beans for 4-6 mins or until just tender.

STEP 3

Push the onion mixture to one side in the pan. Lift the steaks from the bowl, shake off any excess marinade, and sear in the pan for 2½-3 mins, turning once, until cooked but still a little pink inside. Pile the beans onto plates and place the steaks on top. Add the beetroot wedges, olives and remaining marinade to the pan and cook briefly to heat through, then spoon on top and around the steaks. Add the rocket and serve.

Chicken & pearl barley risotto

Prep:5 mins **Cook:**40 mins

Serves 2

Ingredients

- 1 tsp sunflower oil
- 2 chicken thighs , skinless, bone in
- 2 carrots , chopped
- 2 celery sticks , chopped
- 1 onion , chopped
- 1 garlic clove , crushed
- 140g pearl barley

For the green dressing

- ½ x 60g bag fresh rocket leaves
- small handful mint , leaves only
- small handful flat-leaf parsley
- juice 1 lemon
- 1 tsp capers

Method

STEP 1

Heat a large saucepan over a medium-high heat and add the oil. Add the chicken and fry for 5 mins or until well-browned on all sides. Tip in the vegetables and cook for a further 5 mins until starting to soften. Add the garlic and pearl barley, then pour over 500ml water. Cover and leave to simmer for 25-30 mins, stirring occasionally.

STEP 2

Meanwhile, put all the dressing ingredients in the small bowl of a food processor and blitz until very finely chopped. Transfer to a bowl and set aside until serving.

STEP 3

When the pearl barley is soft, but still with a little bite, and most of the liquid has been absorbed, it's ready to serve. Season to taste and divide the risotto between two plates, adding spoonfuls of the dressing, to serve.

Low-sugar granola

Prep:10 mins **Cook:**30 mins - 35 mins

Makes 500g

Ingredients

- 200g rolled oats
- 150g bag mixed nuts
- 150g mixed seeds
- 1 orange , zested
- 2 tsp mixed spice
- 2 tsp cinnamon
- 2 tbsp cold pressed rapeseed oil
- 1½ tbsp maple syrup

Method

STEP 1

Heat oven to 160C/140C fan/gas 4. Mix all the ingredients in a bowl with a pinch of salt, then spread out on a baking tray.

STEP 2

Roast for 30-35 mins until golden, pulling the tray out of the oven twice while cooking to give everything a good stir – this will help the granola toast evenly. Leave to cool. Will keep in an airtight container for one month.

Chunky butternut mulligatawny

Prep:25 mins **Cook:**40 mins

Serves 6

Ingredients

- 2 tbsp olive or rapeseed oil
- 2 onions , finely chopped
- 2 dessert apples , peeled and finely chopped
- 3 celery sticks, finely chopped
- ½ small butternut squash , peeled, seeds removed, chopped into small pieces
- 2-3 heaped tbsp gluten-free curry powder (depending on how spicy you like it)
- 1 tbsp ground cinnamon
- 1 tbsp nigella seeds (also called black onion or kalonji seeds)
- 2 x 400g cans chopped tomatoes

- 1 ½l gluten-free chicken or vegetable stock
- 140g basmati rice
- small pack parsley , chopped
- 3 tbsp mango chutney , plus a little to serve, if you like (optional)
- natural yogurt , to serve

Method

STEP 1

Heat the oil in your largest saucepan. Add the onions, apples and celery with a pinch of salt. Cook for 10 mins, stirring now and then, until softened. Add the butternut squash, curry powder, cinnamon, nigella seeds and a grind of black pepper. Cook for 2 mins more, then stir in the tomatoes and stock. Cover with a lid and simmer for 15 mins.

STEP 2

By now the vegetables should be tender but not mushy. Stir in the rice, pop the lid back on and simmer for another 12 mins until the rice is cooked through. Taste and add more seasoning if needed. Stir through the parsley and mango chutney, then serve in bowls with yogurt and extra mango chutney on top, if you like.

Creamy leek & bean soup

Prep:10 mins **Cook:**20 mins

Serves 4

Ingredients

- 1 tbsp rapeseed oil
- 600g leeks , well washed and thinly sliced
- 1l hot vegetable bouillon
- 2 x 400g cans cannellini beans , drained
- 2 large garlic cloves , finely grated
- 100g baby spinach
- 150ml full-fat milk

Method

STEP 1

Heat the oil in a large pan, add the leeks and cook on a low-medium heat for 5 mins. Pour in the bouillon, tip in the beans, cover and simmer for 10 mins.

STEP 2

Stir in the garlic and spinach, cover the pan and cook for 5 mins more until the spinach has wilted but still retains its fresh green colour.

STEP 3

Add the milk and plenty of pepper, and blitz with a stick blender until smooth. Ladle into bowls and chill the remainder.